# Improving Workplace Learning

Issues of workplace learning are not specific to particular national contexts, and are topical across the Western world. This can be seen at the level of national and international policy and also in the developing practices of employers, training providers, and trade unions. *Improving Workplace Learning* investigates a variety of workplace contexts and significantly advances knowledge about workplace learning by providing evidence from a variety of organizations to show how workplace learning can be improved. An accessible overview of the key debates in workplace learning, brought to life with illustrations from a range of workplaces in both the public and private sectors, *Improving Workplace Learning* is a unique and broad-ranging text.

This important new addition to the Improving Learning series is grounded on a range of rich and detailed empirical studies. Focusing on guidelines for improving learning, the text marries the very best theory and practice to provide an accessible and authoritative guide to workplace learning. Practitioners, policymakers, students, and academics with an interest in learning at work will find this an invaluable addition to their bookshelves.

**Karen Evans** is Professor of Education (Lifelong Learning) at the Institute of Education, University of London and Co-Director of the Centre for Excellence in Work-Based Learning for Education Professionals. **Phil Hodkinson** is Professor of Lifelong Learning at the School of Education, University of Leeds. **Helen Rainbird** is Professor of Human Resource Management at the Birmingham Business School, University of Birmingham. **Lorna Unwin** is Professor of Vocational Education and Head of Department at the Centre for Labour Market Studies, University of Leicester.

# Improving Learning TLRP

Series Editor: Director of the ESRC Teaching and Learning Programme

# Improving Workplace Learning

Karen Evans, Phil Hodkinson,
Helen Rainbird and Lorna Unwin

with Alison Fuller, Heather
Hodkinson, Natasha Kersh,
Anne Munro and Peter Senker

Routledge
Taylor & Francis Group

LONDON AND NEW YORK

First published 2006
by Routledge
2 Park Square, Milton Park, Abingdon Oxon OX14 4RN

Simultaneously published in the USA and Canada
by Routledge
270 Madison Ave, New York, NY 10016

*Routledge is an imprint of the Taylor and Francis Group, an informa business*

© 2006 Karen Evans, Phil Hodkinson, Helen Rainbird and Lorna Unwin

Typeset in Charter ITC and StoneSans by
Keystroke, Jacaranda Lodge, Wolverhampton
Printed and bound in Great Britain by
TJ International Ltd, Padstow, Cornwall

*British Library Cataloguing in Publication Data*
A catalogue record for this book is available from the British Library

*Library of Congress Cataloging in Publication Data*
Improving learning at work / Karen Evans . . . [et al.].
        p. cm.
    Includes bibliographical references and index.
    1. Organizational learning.  2. Knowledge management.
    3. Employees—Training of.  I. Evans, Karen, 1949–
    HD58.82.I465 2006
    658.3′124—dc22                                    2005035870

ISBN10: 0–415–37119–8 (hbk)
ISBN10: 0–415–37120–1 (pbk)

ISBN13: 978–0–415–37119–3 (hbk)
ISBN13: 978–0–415–37120–9 (pbk)

# Contents

**PART III**
**The Conclusions** 161

# Illustrations

## Figures

## Boxes

## Tables

# Series editor's preface

The Improving Learning series showcases findings from projects within ESRC's Teaching and Learning Research Programme (TLRP)—the UK's largest ever coordinated educational research initiative.

Books in the Improving Learning series are explicitly designed to support "evidence-informed" decisions in educational practice and policymaking. In particular, they combine rigorous social and educational science with high awareness of the significance of the issues being researched.

Working closely with practitioners, organizations, and agencies covering all educational sectors, the programme has supported many of the UK's best researchers to work on the direct improvement of policy and practice to support learning. Over sixty projects have been supported, covering many issues across the lifecourse. We are proud to present the results of this work through books in the Improving Learning series.

Each book provides a concise, accessible, and definitive overview of innovative findings from a TLRP investment. If more advanced information is required, the books may be used as a gateway to academic journals, monographs, websites, etc. On the other hand, shorter summaries and research briefings on key findings are also available via the programme's web site at <http://www.tlrp.org>.

We hope that you will find the analysis and findings presented in this book helpful to you in your work on improving outcomes for learners.

Andrew Pollard
Director, Teaching and Learning Research Programme
Institute of Education, University of London

# Preface and acknowledgements

Across the Western world, there is a growing awareness of the importance of the workplace as a site for learning. This can be seen at the level of national and international policy (including the European Union [EU]) and also in the developing practices of employers, training providers, and trade unions.

This Gateway book is based on the research carried out through one of the Economic and Social Research Council (ESRC) Teaching and Learning Research Programme's (TLRP) "research networks." The Networks, funded in Phase I of the TLRP, were important innovations within the wider program. In the case of the Network on "Improving Incentives to Learning in the Workplace," our approach has been distinctive. Rather than working as a team on one coordinated project, there were five projects that made up the Network, each with its own small research team, and each with its own specific research focus. Our focus was to develop research that could help improve learning in workplaces, with the following objectives:

1   To develop an interdisciplinary understanding of the context of workplace learning, which is characterized by the conflict embodied in the wage relationship and wider systems for the management and regulation of employment.
2   To explore and develop learning theory in relation to the pedagogy of the workplace.
3   To test and refine contemporary theories of "apprenticeship" in a variety of contexts.
4   To develop a better understanding of the practice of learning at, for, and through the workplace, leading to the development of a concept of apprenticeship as a model of contemporary workplace teaching and learning.

5   To build capacity in this under-researched field.

6   To contribute to improved practice amongst a range of practitioners whose activities affect teaching and learning in the workplace and, in some cases, in formal educational contexts as well.

The five projects were:

Project 1  The Regulatory Framework of the Employment Relationship (Rainbird/Munro).

Project 2  Recognition of Tacit Skills and Knowledge in Work Re-entry (Evans/Kersh).

Project 3  The Workplace as a Site for Learning: Opportunities and Barriers in Small and Medium-sized Enterprises (Fuller/ Unwin).

Project 4  An Exploration of the Nature of Apprenticeship as a Site for Learning in an Advanced Economy (Senker).

Project 5  The School as a Site for Workplace Learning (Hodkinson/ Hodkinson).

The five projects explored, in and through real work settings, theories and concepts relevant to learning at work, including situated learning, communities of practice, apprenticeship as a model of learning, informal learning, and tacit skills. The Network included a wide range of workers and organizations in the research, with the aim of producing well-founded and widely applicable results:

- young recruits, adult returners, and ongoing experienced workers;
- public and private sectors;
- occupations ranging from routine and manual jobs to professional occupations;
- predominantly male, predominantly female, and mixed-gender occupations.

Each project developed from the particular interests and disciplinary backgrounds of the principal researchers involved. The varied expertise of the team has enabled us to bring inter-disciplinary perspectives to our analysis and theoretical development. The way in which we have developed this Gateway book has been consistent with the overall network approach. While responsibility for each chapter has been taken by one or two "lead authors," the approaches and analyses are essentially collaborative and the outcomes integrated. The methodology is described in detail in the Methodology Appendix.

Practitioners, employers, policymakers, and other stakeholders have been involved throughout the research process. We are particularly grateful to Jim Sutherland, the former Director of Education and Training at UNISON, and chair of the Government's Workplace Learning Task Group (1997–8), who acted as Practitioner Advisor. Our Advisory Group members also played key roles: Richard Banks (TOPSS England), Donald Cameron (UNISON), Ian Carnell (Engineering and Marine Training Authority), Bert Clough (TUC), Helen Hill (NUT), Peter Hill (Steel Training Limited), Maria Hughes (Learning and Skills Development Agency), John Monniot (Teaching Company Directorate), Andrew Schumm (Swindon Pressings Limited), and John Stevens (CIPD). We are grateful to all for the advice they offered and assistance they gave in different ways. Each project benefited from collaboration with and contributions from relevant practitioners. We thank all of the people who helped us gain access to a wide range of research sites and all of those who participated in the research process. There are too many people to name here, but without the generosity of the employees, in all our research sites, who gave up their time to talk to us, we would not have been able to produce the range of evidence presented in this book. Our thanks also go to Pam Gellatly for her patience and hard work in wordprocessing the manuscript.

The analysis and findings have also been informed by debate and discussion with our research colleagues in, for example, the ESRC Teaching and Learning Research Programme, the European network VETNET, the ESRC Centre for Skills Knowledge and Organizational Performance (SKOPE) at the universities of Oxford and Warwick, and the National Institute of Adult Continuing Education (NIACE). Parts of Chapters 4 and 5 are based upon the article, "The Significance of Individual Biography in Workplace Learning," published in *Studies in the Education of Adults*, 36 (1) 6–26. Parts of that paper are reproduced here, with the editor's permission.

The book is intended to be of use to students, practitioners, policy-makers, and researchers who are interested in the phenomenon of workplace learning. In presenting research evidence from a variety of workplace contexts, the book offers a unique combination of breadth of coverage and depth of understanding. It is hoped that the book will contribute to improvements in the ways in which organizations and policymakers develop their own understandings of the relationship between workplace learning and the contextual factors that advance or hinder such learning.

As with other books in the Gateway series, the main groups of intended readers are people who can put the ideas into practice, including human-resource (HR) professionals; the providers of workplace learning, including private training organizations and colleges; trade-union officials and officers with a responsibility for learning; and policymakers and policy-influencing groups with a remit for promoting lifelong learning and workforce development. We also believe that academics researching in the field of workplace learning will find this a useful summary of the Network's research and an access point for further information. The book is grounded in a range of rich and detailed empirical studies. It suggests ways for improving learning in relation to significant theoretical advances.

We believe the book will be of interest at an international level as issues of workplace learning are not specific to particular national contexts and are topical across different societies and policy contexts. By focusing in parts of the book on the UK policy context, we hope to have shown that workplace learning has to take serious account of the impact of policymaking, and, as such, hope that readers in other countries can use some of our analytical devices to examine the relationship between policy and learning in their own situations.

Karen Evans, Phil Hodkinson, Helen Rainbird, and Lorna Unwin

# Part I

# The Issues

# Chapter 1

# Workplace learning
## Perspectives and challenges

## Introduction

The research on which this book is based has aimed to examine learning within the socioeconomic context of the workplace. The conflict embodied in the wage relationship and wider systems for the management and regulation of employment frame our exploration of workplace learning. The improvement of workplace learning requires a critical examination of what is currently provided and the structures and regulatory framework within which it takes place. It also requires an understanding of how workers learn, as individuals and collectively. Our evidence, from employers and employees in many, varied workplaces in the private and public sector, has led us toward integrated and culturally embedded approaches to the improvement of workplace learning. In this chapter, we begin this process by considering the potential and limits of workplace learning, and the contemporary theories that can shed light on the practices of learning in, for and through the workplace.

## Workplace learning: Potential and limits

The idea that learning is critical to economic success has been around for a long time. Since the mid-nineteenth century, British governments have been concerned about the relative weakness of vocational training and its influence on the performance of the economy relative to that of competitor nations, and these concerns have been echoed in the twentieth century (Perry 1976). This has been intensified since the oil crisis of the 1970s and the perception of the pervasiveness of globalization as an inexorable force affecting national economies. In most instances, this has been seen in terms of improvements in formal education and

*Lead authors: Karen Evans and Helen Rainbird*

training. This book deals with the broader subject of workplace learning as an activity which is embedded in the production process and the social interactions of the workplace, as well as more formal learning interventions related to the work environment.

In the light of these developments in the economy, there is now a perception that Fordist forms of work organization, based on F. W. Taylor's principles of reducing the skill requirements of the production process through the specialization of work tasks, need to be replaced by ones requiring higher levels of worker skills and organizational commitment. This has taken various forms, ranging from Piore and Sabel's (1984) model of "flexible specialization" and Kern and Schumann's (1984) "new production concepts" in Germany, to different national models of human-resource management (HRM): The Anglo-US model, the European model/s, and the Japanese (see Harzing and Van Ruysseveldt 2004). This has been accompanied by a discourse about the need for companies to become "learning organizations" (Senge 1990, Pedlar et al. 1991) and to engage in "knowledge management" (see Scarborough et al. 1998 for a review). The key point to emerge is that in a global economy where companies can switch locations to take advantage of the benefits of low wage costs, there is a view that the qualifications and skills of the workforce need to be raised so that the high wage costs of production facilities in the developed world can be justified. This applies not only to the formal qualifications of young people leaving the education system and starting their careers, but also to workers already in employment. Existing employees need to increase their skills and adapt to changes in work organization and technology and, at the same time, to improve their wider employability in the labor market, in the event of redundancy.

In the UK, the centrality of lifelong learning to both economic success and social inclusion has been emphasized, as in the Green Paper *The Learning Age. A Renaissance for a New Britain* (DfEE 1998). More importantly, for our argument, it emphasized the significance of the workplace both as a site of learning and as a site of access to learning. These two strands of argument come together in suggesting that new approaches to managing labor presuppose an increased requirement for workers to develop their skills and qualifications in order for companies to be successful in the new business environment, on the one hand; and that there is a need for the workplace to be developed as a site for accessing different forms of learning, on the other.

Despite the recognition of the need for learning at work and the potential of the workplace as a site of learning, serious questions are raised about the extent to which this potential can be realized in practice. Research evidence suggests that many companies are not engaged in the types of market strategies that require higher levels of workforce skills and learning. These strategies include: A continuing preference for cost-based competition and a reliance on the production of standardized goods and services, hierarchical management structures and low trust relationships, and limited scope for developing environments in which creativity and innovation are encouraged (Keep and Rainbird 2000: 190). Where companies attempt to align their HRM strategies more closely to their business strategies, this can take different forms. As Storey argues, the "hard" version of HRM emphasizes "the quantitative, calculative and business-strategic aspects of managing the headcounts resource in a rational way as for any other economic factor." In contrast, the "soft" version, with its roots in the Human Relations school of management, emphasizes "communication, motivation and leadership" (1989: 8). Where labor is treated as a disposable factor of production, employers are unlikely to invest in skill development, and work is likely to be designed in ways that reduce rather than enhance the scope for workplace learning. Skill-enhancement strategies are more likely to be found in the "soft" version of HRM.

## Locating workplace learning in the employment relationship

The employment relationship is significant to workplace learning because the workplace is a site where workers experience the unequal power relations between themselves and the employer. Although much of the policy debate assumes that what is good for business is also good for employees and for society, writers in the field of industrial relations make the distinction between the unitary and pluralist views of the employment relationship (Fox 1966). The unitary (or unitarist) framework is one that sees employers and employees as sharing an identity of interests. In contrast, the pluralist framework sees conflict at work as inevitable, because workers and managers have different interests and power bases. As a consequence, securing workers' consent is not an automatic process but an uncertain and insecure one that needs to be achieved through active management (Edwards 2003: 12). Edwards argues that the key point about the

> indeterminacy of the labour contract and strategies of labour control is that managers and workers are locked into a relationship

that is contradictory and antagonistic. It is contradictory . . . because managements have to pursue the objectives of control and releasing creativity, both of which are inherent in the relationship with workers and which call for different approaches.

(2003: 16)

This is the context of workplace learning and workplace-learning interventions, which are, in turn, constitutive of the employment relationship.

The point here is that the workplace is a site in which antagonistic relationships are expressed, but may also involve a degree of cooperation and the establishment of consensus. This has consequences both for the relationship between managers and their employees, including trade unions if they are present in the workplace. In a discussion of new forms of work organization, Geary (1995) argues that two positions have been adopted. The optimistic position takes the view that management

are no longer content to rely merely in securing employees' compliance through a narrow conception of the labour contract, but seek instead to win over employees' hearts and minds by developing broad job descriptions, encouraging greater flexibility and engendering employees' involvement in the affairs of the enterprise.

(1995: 369)

In contrast, the pessimistic view is that "management are more concerned to root out shopfloor challenges to their right to manage than to transform the manner in which work is organized" (Geary 1995: 370). As a consequence, "the assumption that new structures of work organization will engender harmony in place of adversarial relations must be viewed sceptically" (Hyman and Streeck 1988: 4).

## From "training" to "workplace learning"

Whereas earlier debates on learning at and for work tended to focus on initial education and vocational training, there has been a shift of emphasis in the UK to learning and skills. This reflects and is reflected in changing institutional structures. Whereas in the 1960s and 1970s, the structures were the industrial-training boards (ITBs) and the Manpower Services Commission (MSC), by the beginning of the twenty-first century, this had shifted to the Learning and Skills Council (LSC) (via the training and enterprise councils [TECs]). Nevertheless, the link between skills and work organization is significant, as is the shift in vocabulary of policy documents from "training" to "workplace learning." For whereas training implies an intervention which is formally structured and involves the transfer of a body of knowledge, workplace learning is more encompassing and involves locating learning in social relations at work. Although this can take a variety of forms, it is significant that informal learning is acquiring an increasing profile in EU policy documents (European Commission 2001), and this is reflected in the concern of organizations such as the Chartered Institute of Personnel and Development (CIPD) with "capability frameworks."

If we adopt the definition of the Workplace Learning Task Group (which reported to the National Advisory Group on Continuing Education and Lifelong Learning), it refers to "that learning which derives its purpose from the context of employment" (Sutherland 1998: 5). This goes beyond training, which is narrowly focused on the immediate task and restricted to business needs, but involves "learning in, through and for the workplace." In adopting this broader definition of workplace learning, it explicitly addresses the learning needs of a variety of stakeholders in the workplace: Employees, potential employees, and government, in addition to those of employers.

*Learning in the workplace* can refer to a variety of different forms of learning which may or may not be formally structured, some of which take place spontaneously through the social interactions of the workplace. Eraut et al.'s (1998) research on highly qualified workers points to a variety of ways in which people say they learn: By observing others, through mentoring arrangements, by making mistakes. A key point here is the extent to which the organization of production affords opportunities for learning. Whereas the highly qualified workers studied by Eraut et al. had many opportunities for learning, which arose through the high level of work autonomy they experienced, this is not the case for all workers. Those who define their work as "boring" and "monotonous" and who experience job deskilling may have few intrinsic opportunities for learning at work (Rainbird et al. 1998). Whether or not workers receive formal training in work routines, the workgroup itself may impose rules of acceptable behavior and its boundaries through the socialization process (Seymour 2005, Lewis 2005).

*Learning through the workplace* refers to learning opportunities that are accessed as part of the employment relationship. In other words, this

refers to learning that is accessed by employees through their relationship to the employer. Some employees, such as professional workers,
may have an expectation of access to learning as part of their package
of employment benefits or as a condition of membership of a professional organization. Other workers may not have such expectations.
These entitlements may be obtained through workplace custom and
practice, collective bargaining, or legislation and may refer not only
to learning that is immediately related to the current job, but also to
broader development opportunities and wider employability.

*Learning for the workplace* refers to learning opportunities that may
be narrowly or broadly defined. An example of the former would be
job-related training, and an example of the latter would be general
education, which may be directly or indirectly related to the job.
Whereas the former could be considered as an example of training for
*employer need*, the latter represents an example of training for *employee
need*, whereby a worker gains access to learning that contributes to their
broader development and skills or contributes to their understanding
of their role and function within the wider organization (Rainbird et al.
2003).

## The ESRC Research Network: Improving incentives to learning at work

The research on which this book is based sought to examine learning
within the socioeconomic context of the workplace, with a focus on its
inherent tensions and unequal power relations. It aimed to develop an
interdisciplinary understanding of the context of workplace learning,
which was understood as being characterized by the conflict embodied
in the wage relationship and wider systems for the management and
regulation of employment. It aimed to explore and develop learning
theory in relation to the pedagogy of the workplace and to test and
refine contemporary theories of "apprenticeship" in a variety of contexts.
Finally, it aimed to develop a better understanding of the practice
of learning at, for and through the workplace and to analyze critically
the concept of apprenticeship as a model of contemporary workplace
teaching and learning. It did this by exploring a range of different
sites of learning, examining the experiences of young recruits, adult
returners, and experienced workers in the public and private sectors.
The occupations studied ranged from the so-called "unskilled" to professional and included a sample of predominantly male, predominantly
female and mixed-gender occupations.

In the course of the Network's research, interviews were conducted with 230 learners/employees of whom fifty-five were longitudinally tracked within or between sites of learning. A total of 170 questionnaires and 281 learning logs were completed by research participants. Ten colleges/training providers and forty-one workplace sites were researched, including private- and public-sector organizations, school departments, small and medium enterprises (SMEs), service providers' sites, work placement and Teaching Company Scheme (TCS) sites.[1] Observations were carried out during more than 250 days of site visits, and interviews were conducted with 116 key informants (tutors, trainers, managers, employers, officers and representatives of trade-union and employer organizations, officers of sectoral training bodies).

Our research shows that attempts to improve workplace learning through a predominantly target-driven approach are often counterproductive. Such approaches can be seen in the proliferation of performance-management schemes and short-term training initiatives and provision. The findings emphasize two weaknesses and one omission with such approaches. They are underpinned by a view of learning as the acquisition of skills and knowledge, rather than a more supportable view of workplace learning as participation. As a result, they are often short-term in intended impact and overlook learning which cannot be easily measured. They are undermined because some workers respond through strategic compliance and resistance rather than the enthusiasm intended by managers. They fail to address working practices and conditions of employment as key influences on workplace learning. More fundamentally, our research has contributed to a better understanding of workplace learning in the ways shown in Box 1.1.

## Toward a better understanding of workplace learning

Our focus on the workplace as a site of access to learning, "that learning which derives its purpose from the context of employment" means therefore that our perspectives on *learning in, through, and for the workplace* have to address the needs of a variety of stakeholders:

---

1 Since the research was carried out, the TCS has been retitled Knowledge Transfer Partnerships.

---

**BOX 1.1**

*Rethinking workplace learning: Four contributions*

The research carried under the Network made four specific contributions to the understanding of workplace learning. The first of these was the integration of macro-level analysis with the characteristics of the learning environment, which expands the more normal context for workplace-learning theorizing, which is the workplace itself. Second, the work conducted is at the forefront of a growing international focus* on the integration of individual perspectives into social and cultural understandings of workplace learning. Third, Fuller and Unwin (2004) developed the concept of the expansive–restrictive continuum of workplace learning (discussed in more detail in Chapter 2) as a means of characterizing the quality of the learning environment, which represents an original contribution to theorizing learning in the workplace. Finally, the dispositions and tacit skills of workers influence the nature of the working environment and the ways in which workers react to and interact with that environment. These dimensions are interrelated.

*See the edited collection 'Workplace learning in context' (Rainbird et al. 2004) which was based on an international workshop run as part of the Network and to which members of the research team contributed.

---

Employees, potential employees, employers and government. Since workplaces afford many informal learning opportunities, which result from interactions in workgroups and from the structure of the work environment, one of the challenges of the future is to identify strategies to assist workers who support the learning of others (whether they be teachers, trainers, supervisors, coaches, or managers) to connect their learning to broader frameworks than those offered by their work roles. This will help them to go beyond their immediate context and to appreciate the wider relevance of their work activity and the learning it has fostered.

Over the last decade, the discourses of HRM, the "learning organization" and "knowledge management" would seem to suggest that learning is a central concern in the workplace. Yet the harsh reality of the operating environments of many public-and private-sector organizations means that the rhetoric is not even aspiration let alone a reflection of practice. Indeed, research evidence suggests that there are often significant organizational and cultural barriers to the promotion of individual and organizational learning. These (see Evans and Rainbird 2002) can include:

- cost-based competition;
- standardized products and services;
- a heavy reliance on economy-of-scale advantages;
- low trust relationships;
- hierarchical management structures;
- people-management systems that emphasize command, control and surveillance;
- an underlying belief that (whatever the rhetoric) people are a cost or a disposable factor of production;
- little slack or space for creativity;
- a culture of blame where mistakes (particularly those of lower-status workers) are punished.

The theories that are best fitted, and therefore currently dominant, in the search for better understandings of workplace learning are constructivist and sociocultural theories. These are important because they emphasize the significance of the context and environment for learning. They recognize skill and knowledge as embodied, and they acknowledge the significance of power relations. They consider the tacit as well as the explicit dimensions of skills and knowledge and the ways old knowledge and new can be linked in processes of knowledge construction. These perspectives, taken together, show how people learn through purposeful interaction in social settings and explore ways in which their knowledge and understanding can be further advanced through structured teaching and learning. Our research is using this theoretical basis to develop the longitudinal perspective that these theories have lacked previously, working toward (i) a life-course dimension that links understanding about workplace learning with life-course perspectives; and (ii) developing models for learning and teaching that allow adults in a range of industries and services explicitly to connect their tacit knowledge to their current learning and to work-related processes.

Within the theoretical spectrum of approaches to workplace learning, socioanthropological perspectives have overtaken behaviorist and humanistic/experiential approaches in the search for better understandings of the complexities of workplace learning. These came significantly into the frame in the 1990s with Lave and Wenger's (1991) and Wenger's (1999) studies of "situated cognition" and the ways in which skills were constructed, recognized, and ascribed value in workplace environments and communities of practice. This social process of learning can be considered as a gradual process of growing participation in communities of practice, which originally was seen as a group of experts collaborating to accomplish a common aim (Lave and Wenger 1991). According to this concept, learning is a simultaneous process of belonging (to a community of practice), of becoming (developing an identity as member of this community), of experiencing (the meaning of the common work task), and of doing (as practical action contributing to the common work task) (Wenger 1999: 5). While this social theory of learning was developed with regard to learning in contexts considered by some to be very far removed from the workplaces of modern (post-industrial) societies such as Britain, many have built on this ethnographic research and obtained from it insights important not only for understanding learning in professional and workplace communities, but also for rethinking how social and vocational disengagement occurs and how people may be "reconnected" through situated learning (see Evans and Niemeyer 2004). Although the empirical foundations on which the theories of situated cognition are based come from contexts that differ substantially from those which shape many contemporary work-based programs, these perspectives on situated learning have undoubtedly offered new ways of thinking about workplace learning. However the concepts have become overstretched as they have been seized on by researchers trying to explain and theorize phenomena that meet few of the underlying assumptions of the original theory (see Hodkinson and Hodkinson 2004, Fuller and Unwin 2003a, Evans and Niemeyer 2004 for a fuller discussion).

While theories of situated learning appeared promising in offering the potential for more holistic formulations of workplace learning that go beyond the parallel tracks of vocational and social pedagogy, we have worked toward an expanded set of constructs that differ from Lave and Wenger's concepts in some significant respects, to address the particular characteristics of workplace learning in contemporary apprenticeships and for adults in the pressured and changing contexts of, for example, SMEs, contracting out, and the often troubled or interrupted processes of transition between learning and working environments.

Our constructs highlight the following features, while recognizing the socially situated nature of the learning:

- The individual biography of each person is highly significant for their engagement in the learning environments and "communities" in question.
- Workplace learning that does not take place in closed communities may have the goal of enabling people to "move through" and to "move on."
- The concepts of "novice" and "expert" do not have the same salience: Newcomers bring capabilities with them, they participate, move through, and eventually move on with strengthened capabilities, which they share on the way. Expert status in this context comes with the responsibilities for creating and maintaining the environment for full participation.

Our expanded concepts of situated learning encompass these features. Ensuring the engagement of people, whether apprentices or experienced workers, in the intended learning is often the single biggest challenge for educators and trainers, since without engagement there is no motivation and no learning. Expanded concepts of situated learning have viewed learning as situated in three ways:

- in practical activity;
- in the culture and context of the workplace/learning environment;
- in the sociobiographical features of the learners' life.

Learning that is situated practically involves:

- engagement in actual work practices and work groups;
- access to programs of activity;
- the time and space provided for learning.

Learning that is situated culturally is consistent with:

- the history and culture of vocational education and training (VET) in the organization and area;
- the working milieu in general.

To be situated socially/biographically requires:

- shared responsibility for learning and personal development;
- the adjustment of the learning context to learners' interests and experiences;
- links between activities and chains of support;
- the acknowledgement of social and emotional dimensions of learning.

Evidence suggests that learning has to be well situated in each of these ways for full engagement to occur (see Evans 2002c). It is commonly held that forms of learning that go beyond mere technical qualification considerably help to increase the motivation of adults and young people for education and training. Participation in a work process potentially encourages taking on responsibility and develops commitment. Practical work in a team can help to make learning success visible and to enable individuals to experience individual contributions to the collective activity as personal success. To have learning in an actual workplace context recognized can highlight the importance of the work. Transnational research (see Heidegger 1997, Illeris 2004) has shown that there is a European-wide shift toward learning methods that relate more strongly to prior and current experiences of social and informal learning and that aim to provide a closer link to the workplace realities.

For adults with interrupted or problematic work histories, the four dimensions of learning identified as "doing, experiencing, belonging, and becoming" are crucial for people at risk of becoming socially disconnected, whether through unemployment, isolation, or alienation. Work and training placements that have a close link to the local labor market can affirm individuals in their value of what they can do, provided they have been chosen properly according to the interests, abilities, and needs of the persons involved. Real rather than simulated workplace settings have shown to be most effective to rebuild the wish to learn. However, the specific context of work entry or reentry, particularly for young people and adults who have experienced difficulties in the labor market, requires a review of the idea of communities of practice. The social theory of situated learning presupposes the community being ready and willing to open for newcomers/learners on the one side and to share the meaning of the common activity and the underlying values on the other. Thus, it appears to be rather idealistic and optimistic. While the ideas of enhancing learning and expanding experience through situating people in various "real-life" environments rightly highlights the social dimensions in the process of learning, there is often insufficient analysis of how mechanisms of power and hierarchy, selection, and exclusion also operate in real-life environments.

Our research has aimed to consider the needs and situations of specific groups of employees and potential employees, with their individual histories, abilities, and career orientations. Some, but not all have been involved in various forms of the mainstream vocational/ professional education and training on offer. We have sought holistic ways of understanding learning as the processes by which human capacities are expanded, in, for, and through the workplace. These processes require a balance to be struck between the challenges of actual workplace contexts and the time, space, and support necessary for learning to be deep and satisfying.

## Situated learning and competence development

Theories of learning have been developed predominantly with the perspective on established learning settings. But in many cases these are exactly the settings of learning in which people have previously experienced failure, which means that they are not the best places for positive engagement or for forging new senses of themselves or their abilities. We have seen that the concept of situated learning questions the school, college, or training centre as the unique or main conduit for learning in people's lives by valuing informal ways of learning and stressing the importance of other learning surroundings.

Situated approaches to learning recognize the importance of work experience and practical action for the enhancement of processes of learning and understanding. While these are common elements in traditional theories of VET, situated learning theories shift the focus from the individual to the social components of learning. The concepts of situated learning allow for an extended view on competences and competence development. Situated learning is not about specialized training of single skills but about experience and capacities developed through participation. This includes the process of acquiring the cultural attributes of participation: Values and beliefs, common stories, and collective problem-solving strategies. It thereby offers an enhanced view of competences, embodying the mental, emotional, and physical processes that are integral to the development and expansion of human capacities.

In VET programs such as apprenticeship, an important socializing task exists alongside (and entwined with) the processes of vocational skill and knowledge formation. Within the apprenticeship "tradition," not only vocational skills are imparted, the promotion of social competence and personality-building activities are of just as great importance. While "normal" VET particularly aims at the achievement of occupation-specific and technical qualifications, programs must go above and beyond technical qualifications, to offer as broad a vocational orientation as possible. An holistic education is needed to enable young people successfully to take up, continue with, and succeed in an occupation. As important as vocational skills development is the chance to grow in a learning community centered on practice, and to support the young persons on their way to full participation in the various, often overlapping, communities in which they engage. In theory, as in practice, learning and socialization are difficult to separate. Learning is not only an individual act; learning processes are emergent from the social contexts in which they are situated. Learning is therefore not only a question of knowledge transfer but rather it is about allowing young persons to participate in social situations where they are accepted as members who bring new knowledge and skills and have the potential of growing competence.

The balance between vocational instruction by VET professionals and social construction of competences by young persons varies widely, influencing the designs of programs in practice and the role and importance given to the educational staff. When learning is viewed as social interaction in a learning community, thus valuing the social components in learning, the conventional relationship between teachers and learners is questioned. Learning cannot be understood as a one-way or even a two-way process, but instead it has to be viewed as a common activity. This is a special challenge for further-and adult-education programs that aim to embrace work-based pedagogies, because the teachers' role will be revised considerably. Teachers and trainers need to fulfill new roles such as tutors, coaches, advisers, and mediators, and it is important to develop suitable training conditions to enable them to meet these new professional challenges.

Competence development for the adult employee is just as significant. Adult workers are potentially involved in all aspects of learning in, through, and for the workplace. Learning *in* the workplace involves engaging with and mastering changing tasks, roles, and environments; learning *through* the workplace takes place when adults access learning opportunities through their place of work, whether in the form of external courses leading to qualifications, personal-development, adult-education programs or activities accessed through their trade unions. Opportunities for learning *for* the workplace are of particular significance for those who are seeking to reenter the workforce after periods away caused by unemployment, family commitments, or health reasons. All of these forms of learning involve competence development in its "maximal" sense. Maximal versions of competence emphasize underlying generative capacities and regard competence as holistic and contextualized, in contrast to the "minimal" versions, which tended to reduce competence to specific behaviors. These latter approaches predominated in the earliest stages of the UK National Vocational Qualifications (NVQ) framework, as discussed further in Chapter 7.[2]

In task, role, and job change, the ways in which "transfer" of learning occurs between settings and activities is a particular focus of research and debate. The idea that transfer can take place at all is contested in understandings of situated learning modeled on Lave and Wenger, who argue that learning is so embedded in, and part of, the specific workplace culture and context that "transfer" has no meaning. However, it is self-evident that adults do carry their learning between settings and activities in complex ways. Understanding these ways better has been a particular focus for researchers such as Eraut (2004) and Billett (2004). For example, Eraut uses the metaphor of an iceberg, with codified knowledge gained from extended courses of professional preparation as the "tip" above the surface of the water. He argues that further learning and practice are required to convert this into the personal knowledge that is ready for use in a range of work situations. The underlying personal knowledge is symbolized by the mass of ice lying invisibly below the surface, the larger and more significant part of the structure. Much of this learning is tacit, minimal support is given to it, and its very existence is often denied. From a different starting point, Evans, Kersh and Sakamoto (2004) have also shown that the personal, tacit competences that adults have already gained through prior learning are frequently neglected but can be very significant in role-change situations.

Adult learning in and through workplaces is both active and related to the "affordances" of the workplace, that is, the activities and guidance that individuals can access. Billett, in exploring the experiences of adult workers, concludes that "individuals' agency determines how what

---

workplaces afford is construed and judged worthy of participation" (2004: 117).

In our research, the experiences of professionals, new entrants, and experienced workers in a range of occupations are analyzed in order to explore the potential and limits of various aspects of situated learning more thoroughly.

## Limitations and potential of situated learning concepts

The concept of situated learning itself is socially situated. If applied uncritically, it can help to serve the strategies of new qualification policies that are exclusively dominated by workplace and employers' demands, neglecting the role and responsibility of the established providers of education. The dangers of this are self-evident: That the long-term weaknesses of VET will be intensified rather than solved by such arguments and strategies, as shown in the European-wide 2004 study by Evans and Niemeyer. It has also been argued that situated learning involving "legitimate peripheral participation" (Lave and Wenger 1991) does not allow for the individual to grow beyond the borders of the respective community of practice or to take a critical position toward it. Experience with the apprenticeship model in vocational education also adds to this critique. To have novice and expert regularly working together in an authentic context does not automatically produce a learning process. Apprentices are not always accepted as legitimate members of the community of practice. Their positions as learners can also be limited in practice. Apart from all the positive experiences recorded in evaluation studies (see Fuller and Unwin 2002, for example), this environment does not guarantee learning. The rights of full access to a conventional community of craft practice can be reduced by hierarchies and the balance of power within the group. Moreover, many "workplace learners" have continuing needs for learning support beyond the immediate communities of practice. And the aim for some will be to move on and through the community, rather than from "novice" to "expert" status within it. Increasing engagement, gains in social confidence, and a growing range of skills mark this process.

Our expanded concepts of situated learning have to include the question of the critical dimension of participation and the direction of the learning processes in a learning community centered on practice. When participation includes the right to criticize and the ability to learn how to criticize constructively, the participant can influence and contribute to shaping the values and strategies within the team or work group. While this principle can apply in a learning community centered on practice that is explicitly designed for the purposes of learning and creativity, as often applies in the case of "knowledge workers," it is obviously difficult to realize in work environments with command-and-control management strategies.

Some conventional 1 systems have a strong selective function that can hamper weaker learners' progress. Pedagogical approaches that aim to build on strengths by nurturing biographical and tacit competences often suffer from insufficient recognition. How can these capabilities and progress in their development be acknowledged, recognized, and built on in workplaces? There are theoretical and practical challenges for these approaches, but, as we show in Chapter 4, they show considerable potential for first understanding and then improving learning. These approaches recognize that the majority of workplace learning is informal and is best understood through initially examining the relationship between the learner (taking into account his or her prior learning), the practical work activities available in the job and work environment, and the cultural and social relations of the workplace. In order to use research to effect improvements in learning, this conceptualization needs to be closely linked to the realities of contrasting and diverse workplaces.

Throughout the book, we use these ideas to explore how they may intersect to produce better understandings of workplace-learning processes and to uncover the extent to which strategies to increase incentives to learn are themselves situation-specific or generalizable.

## Linking workplace learning with further and higher education

While workplace learning has long been associated with college-based further education, in apprenticeships incorporating day release or block release, a rather different concept, that of "work-based learning," gained in momentum and was taken up in higher-education policy discourses in the late 1980s and early 1990s. In the UK, the Department of Employment defined work-based learning as, "The effective learning that can take place at the workplace, and not only in the formal academic setting of the lecture theatre and laboratory, and help individuals to learn through the experience of work itself" (ED 2006).

This concept is obviously much narrower than our concepts of workplace learning as learning *in, for*, and *through* the workplace. It is centered on the problematic interface between theoretical, "classroom-based" learning and the learning through practice that takes place in the work placement or workshop/laboratory environment. Nevertheless, the workplace experience of the block-release or professional-year student also exposes the learner to at least some of the wider aspects of workplace learning, either directly or by observation, although the placements do not embody many of the features of the employer–employee relationships that are so crucial in influencing workplace learning experiences.

The idea that learning based on work activities could be integrated into, and possibly accredited within, academic programs was a controversial one within higher education. The notion that such learning is "valid and creditworthy" was, as Guile (2005) has argued, a clear departure from conventional higher-education thinking and practice. In the main, universities had retained the tradition of separating theory and practice and rarely offered accreditation for the latter within the structure of degree programs (Barnett 1994). In the early 1990s, these debates about 'work-based learning' in higher education were centered, in the UK, on the potential and limitations of the National Council for Vocational Qualifications (NCVQ) concept of competence, discussed further in Chapter 7. Assessment became a preoccupation, with specialists such as Alison Wolf fiercely critical of the idea that "competent" performance of various functions in the workplace could be taken as sufficient evidence of understanding of the relevant "underpinning" principles and bodies of knowledge (see Black and Wolf 1990).

The original concept of 'work-based learning' has subsequently been shown to be far too narrow to embrace either the diversity of the forms of learning that occurred in the workplace or to address the complex relationship between theory and practice (see for example Barnett 1994, Evans et al. 2002, Rainbird et al. 2004).

Our wider concept of workplace learning focuses attention on its value for organizational development as well as lifelong learning, of which the learning for "employability" of new entrants is only one element. The need for deeper research-based insights into learning at, for, and through the workplace was a conclusion from the ESRC Learning Society Programme, with Coffield (2000) arguing that much more needs to be known about the key processes of learning as embedded in particular workplaces, in organizational structures and in specific social practices. The 2000 EC review of the state of research into work-related education and training, also pointed to the need not only to "audit" the learning opportunities available, but also to evaluate the particular combinations of education, training, employment, and community contexts that can produce "exceptionally rewarding learning environments" on the one hand, or "sterility, where challenges and a series of mundane experiences lead to little learning" (Brown and Keep 1999: 47).

Critiques of the narrowness of the early thinking about workplace learning, combined with growing interest of policymakers and providers in the field have considerably broadened the way that programmes linking the workplace with college-based learning have subsequently developed in the UK and globally. This applies in higher education (see Boud and Soloman 2001, Winter and Maisch 1996) and more widely in the fields of vocational and professional education and training. Linking workplace learning with a theoretical and practical learning undertaken in the "college of" further- or higher-education is a long-standing challenge that has increased in complexity. Development work on new models for linking learning in the workplace reflects the rising demand for this type of curriculum provision from employers and professional institutes, manifested for example in Teaching Company Schemes of the kind researched by Peter Senker in our research network.

One way to appreciate the diversity of approaches used is through Guile and Young's (1995) "connective" typology. This identifies four models of learning found in vocational programs that include workplace experience as part of the learning program: Reformed learning, combining learning, theorizing practice, and connective learning. The models reflect changing ideas about learning in the workplace. They are analytical rather than descriptive; no specific work-based program necessarily fits neatly into any of the models, and some programs may contain elements of more than one model. They can and do coexist in different institutions and in different countries.

*Combining learning* tries to overcome the traditional divide between theory and practice by providing learners with opportunities to investigate their links by, for example, incorporating such strategies as action research, an institutionally focused study of problem-based learning to address specific work-based concerns. It does not attempt to provide learners with concepts to understand forces external to the workplace that may shape and influence practice. *Theorizing practice*, in Guile and Young's model, refers to the process of systematically reflecting on one's own practice within a set of professional concerns about ethics, values, and procedures. One of the main outcomes and attractions of *theorizing* practice is that it involves discerning alternative or improved ways of resolving professional concerns, often presented in the form of a practical assignment or portfolio. *Partnership learning*, as defined by Guile and Young, emphasizes the formulation of common goals between the provider, employer, and professional institutes which could either be expressed in agreed criteria for professional capability and development or through the involvement of professionals in some way in the accreditation process. *Connective learning* is formulated as an elaboration and extension of the preceding models that overcomes their inherent weaknesses. It attempts to overcome the theory/practice divide in two main ways. First, by conceiving of theory as providing concepts for analyzing the constitution of practice as well as the problems that arise for professionals in their places of work and by conceiving of practice as a resource to rethink theory. Second, by taking the social and organizational context of work more explicitly into account. Unlike the other models for which many examples can currently be found in higher education, the connective model suggests a direction for future development that is consistent with the contextualized understanding of workplace learning developed in this book.

Transformations in the nature of work (such as those evidenced in the ESRC Future of Work Programme), fundamentally affect the learning and skills requirements of jobs and individuals at all levels and the ways in which these requirements can be met. This challenges many of the presuppositions and generalizations about the changing nature of work, skills, and learning. With the starting point that the workplace (whether in a school, college, hospital, or business) is a crucially important site for learning and for access to learning, we are continuing to develop analytical perspectives on workplace learning that take the social and organizational context of work and learning more fully into account, and that explore the intersection of work-based pedagogies that originate from research into how people learn at work with the further- and higher-education pedagogies that are applied to people at work.

With these perspectives, we can view teachers as workers in schools as workplaces, and lecturers as workers in colleges and universities as workplaces as readily as we see trainers and supervisors as workers in businesses as workplaces, as Chapter 5 shows.

## Conclusion

This chapter has introduced perspectives that contribute to improving workplace learning in important ways. The first conceptualizes workplace learning as learning in, for, and through the workplace. It shows how this learning is embedded in production processes and social relations and affected by policy contexts beyond the workplace. The second makes connections between the types of programs that incorporate an element of workplace learning and the nonformal aspects of learning that run through everyday workplace practices, between the workplace and wider life–work relationships and the careers of workers and between theoretical frameworks that can contribute to a better understanding of the social nature of the workplace. The third perspective enables a more iterative relationship between theory and practice to develop, by using theoretical concepts for analyzing the constitution of practice as well as the problems that arise for people in their places of work and for conceiving of practice as a resource to rethink theory and received knowledge. A core commitment of the research is to identify how research outcomes can be used to enhance existing scattered "islands of excellence" (Streeck 1989) in practice and to move toward policies and systems that support excellence and equity in workplace learning consistently and comprehensively.

The tensions between participatory and acquisition views of learning, the lack of engagement between work on learning processes and work on inequalities of access to learning, the failure to combine organizational, individual, and wider socioeconomic perspectives in much current theorizing and practice, and a need to incorporate both on- and off-the-job learning have been recognized and addressed in our search for ways to improve learning at work.

# Part II

# The Findings

# Chapter 2

# Expansive and restrictive learning environments

## Introduction

The primary goal of any workplace is to produce goods and services, but the Network's research has confirmed that it is also an important location for teaching and learning. As Chapter 1 has already indicated, however, there are significant differences in the sectoral and organizational contexts within which workplaces sit. In this regard, the Network's case-study findings illustrate the uneven quality of the learning environments that are being created in workplaces and highlight the important task of making sense of such differences if we are to contribute to improving practice. The purpose of this chapter is to outline how the data on apprentice learning collected in Project 3 generated a conceptual framework that can be used to analyze the nature and quality of different approaches to apprenticeship as well as workforce development and organizational learning environments and cultures more generally.

The chapter is organized in three sections. The first identifies the perspective on learning (Lave and Wenger 1991) which underpinned our apprenticeship and wider network research. It draws attention to some of the limitations Lave and Wenger's theorization poses for understanding the sorts of contemporary sites for apprentice and more experienced employee learning encountered in our project, and in the Network as a whole. The second section introduces the conceptual framework, referred to as the *expansive–restrictive* continuum, which we have developed to analyze and to distinguish between contrasting approaches to apprenticeship. The third section suggests ways in which the framework can be extended to address workforce development as a whole. This chapter provides the basis for a more detailed discussion of the wider application of the expansive–restrictive framework to workforce development and organizational culture.

*Lead authors: Alison Fuller and Lorna Unwin*

## The underpinning theoretical perspective

This chapter adopts an inclusive interpretation of what "counts" as workplace learning. By this, we mean that opportunities for participation (learning) cover those that might be viewed as more formalized and intentional as well as those characterized as incidental (Marsick and Watkins 1990). In this regard, we share the position taken by theorists such as Billett (2001), Eraut et al. (2000) and Beckett and Hager (2002), who reject any notion that learning that takes place in specialist educational institutions is inherently superior to learning that takes place in settings such as the workplace or the home. Indeed Eraut et al. (2000) point out that, in many settings, learners experience a mix of formal and "nonformal" learning approaches. This theme is echoed by Darrah, who highlights the importance of the hidden workplace curriculum: "quite apart from the formal attempts to provide instruction, experiences are structured by the organization of work and the technology used, and those experiences provide a powerful, largely unacknowledged curriculum" (1996: 36).

In a recent review of "informal" learning at work (Fuller et al. 2003), we suggested that the metaphor "learning as participation" has become the dominant approach to understanding workplace learning. A central plank of this idea is that each workplace will offer distinctive opportunities, along quantitative and qualitative dimensions, for employees to learn. Adopting this perspective allows research to address how people learn at work in what appears to be a relatively naturalistic way, through participatory activities such as interactions between employees, undertaking tasks, and through playing their work roles. Underpinning this approach is the conception of learning as a process that is primarily social and situated (Lave and Wenger 1991). A strength of the situated perspective is that it treats learning transfer as problematic. If learning is conceived as a process embedded in particular social activities and relations, it follows that learning cannot straightforwardly be replicated from one situation or context to another. This insight draws attention to the pedagogic value of providing employees participating in off-the-job learning programs with support to help facilitate the transfer process.

Looked at from a more critical standpoint, Lave and Wenger's (1991) theory of learning developed from their analysis of how new entrants learn to become members of a community of practice through the process of legitimate peripheral participation. The focus here is on the journey from the periphery of the community of practice to the mainstream undertaken by newcomers and facilitated through their interactions with more experienced colleagues, and their increasing participation in the activities around which the community is sustained. However, the theory has much less to say about the ongoing learning of experienced workers (see Fuller et al. 2005). Moreover, there has been less emphasis in the situated approach on the ways in which organizational factors (including structure, history, and culture) relate to workplace learning. We would argue that an analysis of such characteristics can shed light on the sorts of opportunities for workplace learning that are available and the barriers to learning that might affect individuals and specific workforce groups. Such issues are clearly important to the development of a better understanding of the opportunities open to older workers and their ongoing experiences of learning at work.

Cultural historical activity theory can provide one starting point for addressing the shortcomings in the situated approach. For example, Engeström (2001) identifies how activity theory has evolved from its concentration on individuals to a focus on systems, which are conceived as having internal contradictions and multiple perspectives and voices, and as interacting with other activity systems. Some workplace-learning researchers are recognizing the importance of context and, in particular, the relevance of how work is organized and jobs are designed and distributed, to the type of learning opportunities available to workers (see, *inter alia*, Boud and Garrick 1999, Probert 1999, Koike 1997, 2002). Probert, for example, has argued that the gendered nature of work means that opportunities for and barriers to learning are unevenly dispersed across the workforce. She states that: "there are no grounds for believing that the new emphasis on workplace learning will do anything other than reproduce these inequalities since the dominant discourses continue to rely on abstracted conceptions of work and workers that privilege men" (1999: 113). From another perspective, Solomon (1999) is concerned that the recent emphasis on the opportunity to engage in "informal" learning at work has a negative side in that it may be undermining the need to provide employees with opportunities to engage in off-the-job provision as well. She implies that providing fewer off-the-job opportunities gives employees less chance to stand back and reflect critically on their practice:

> As workplace learning becomes increasingly integrated into everyday work practices and further away from discrete classroom training programmes the socializing of people to be certain kinds

of workers is accompanied by a complementary socialization to be certain kinds of learners.

(Solomon 1999: 123)

Survey research already suggests that employers invest less in training lower-level workers and, consequently, these groups have fewer (formal) training opportunities than their more senior and secure peers (for example, Beinart and Smith 1997, La Valle and Blake 2001). In this regard, we are concerned that the current popularity of situated learning theory is double-edged. On the plus side, as already mentioned, it draws attention to the workplace as an important site for learning. On the other hand, if conceiving all learning as situated has the effect of confining workers to a particular workplace, on the grounds that (all) learning is highly context-dependent, their opportunity to gain new perspectives, to cross boundaries, and to participate in other communities of practice will be denied. It follows that employees' chance to acquire expertise and to engage in the creation of new knowledge will be restricted, and their ability to progress will be inhibited.

In addition, it is important to clarify the relationship between individuals and the opportunities and barriers to learning they may encounter at work. Following Billett (2004), there is a distinction between the extent to which the organizational and pedagogical context affords access to diverse forms of participation and the extent to which individuals "elect to engage" in those opportunities through the exercise of individual agency. The reasons why individuals engage with and respond differently to the (same) workplace learning environment are explained by writers such as Hodkinson and Hodkinson (2004) in terms of individual biographies and dispositions for learning. In her study of adults aged between forty and fifty-six in Australia who embarked on courses of study in their local university after redundancy, Davey (2003) agrees with Cross (1981) that whilst their biographies affect their life-course opportunities, adults can and do still make choices. In our view, it is necessary to recognize the importance of structure in shaping the character and availability of workplace-learning opportunities, whilst at the same time viewing individuals as active agents who can elect the extent to which they engage in the situations open to them.

We have drawn on Lave and Wenger's (1991) theory of "situated learning" to explain the process by which new entrants to an occupation, workplace, or activity progress to becoming full participants in a community of practice. Observation of craft apprenticeships in traditional societies provided the initial empirical inspiration for the concepts of "legitimate peripheral participation" and "communities of practice" that underpin Lave and Wenger's explanation for how novices (apprentices) develop into experts (full participants). While recognizing the relevance of Lave and Wenger's perspective to understanding what is involved in apprenticeship learning, we have focused more specifically on its application to contemporary apprenticeships offered in advanced industrial societies (see Fuller and Unwin 1998, 2003a). We have identified three main shortcomings in the Lave and Wenger account. First, Lave and Wenger downplay the role of formal education institutions in the newcomer's learning process. In the cases investigated by our project, the apprenticeship model includes (to a greater or lesser extent) a combination of formal off-the-job provision as well as the sort of on-the-job learning through participation that forms the central focus of situated learning theory. Second, Lave and Wenger's account does not indicate the relevance of the institutional arrangements, including the nature of the employment relationship, to an analysis of learning in contemporary apprenticeships. Recognition of the importance of the institutional context to the creation of opportunities and barriers to learning is a fundamental concern of our research network. Third, Lave and Wenger conceptualize apprenticeship as a linear journey along which the "novices" learn from their more experienced colleagues. However, we are able to show that young people in contemporary apprenticeships enter the workplace with skills and knowledge which they pass on to more mature workers and, hence, engage in a journey that sees them switching between the role of novice and "expert" according to circumstance.

## Developing and illustrating the expansive–restrictive framework

Through our investigation of apprenticeship, we have hypothesized that apprenticeship learning is likely to have different meanings in different organizational contexts and that the approach taken to apprenticeship will play a key role in shaping those meanings and, therefore, its lived reality (Fuller and Unwin 2003a). Evidence from three companies illustrates the contrasting learning environments being created for apprentices[1] and the opportunities for, and barriers to, learning that ensue.

---

1   The apprentices studies in our project were all participants in the UK government-supported apprenticeship program (known at the time of the research as the Modern Apprenticeship). Details of this program can be found in Fuller and Unwin (2003b).

The companies to which we refer are all associated with the steel industry in England. Company A manufactures bathroom showers and has about 700 employees. It has an extremely well-established apprenticeship program which significantly predates the introduction of the Modern Apprenticeship and which has been used to develop successive generations of skilled and qualified engineers and technicians. Many of the company's ex-apprentices have progressed to senior management positions. Currently, the company employs five apprentices. Of these, three are following apprenticeships in engineering, one in steel production and processing, and one in accountancy. Company B is a small family-run company (around forty employees), which provides steel-polishing services to other businesses. The vast majority of employees work on the factory floor as semiskilled machine operators. The work is managed by the production manager and two company directors. The company offered its first apprenticeships only two years ago as a response to difficulties it was having in recruiting adults with relevant experience. The company currently employs two apprentices who are following the steel industry framework. Company C is a steel "stockholder" with some eighty employees. It is part of a large Swedish corporation but operates as a stand-alone business that buys and sells stainless steel. The workforce is organized into three areas: Sales, administration/finance, and warehouse. This company has no recent experience of offering apprenticeships and only has one apprentice who is training in business administration.

Our project also included a case study in a fourth company (Company D) in Wales. This firm had a history of training apprentices but at the time of the research had suspended its provision due to serious concerns about its ability to survive in difficult trading conditions. Evidence relating to older more experienced workers in Company D will be referred to later in the chapter (see also Fuller and Unwin 2005). This company employed some 300 people and manufactures large steel rods and bars for use in the construction industry.

In Companies B and C, unlike in Company A, there has been no tradition (or perceived need) for employees to gain technical and vocational qualifications alongside their practical experience. Nevertheless, the competitive strategy adopted by the managing director in Company C is heavily focused on improving the quality and efficiency of the company's services. This involves developing a new workplace culture that values individual performance, continuous improvement, innovation, and customer service. To meet these business goals, the company is investing in management-development and customer-service programs largely delivered on site by external consultants. Elsewhere, we have discussed the diverse learning cultures at our case-study companies (Fuller and Unwin 2003a) and have distinguished between strong (expansive) and weak company training and learning cultures.

We have used a range of research methods (including interviews, observations, and weekly learning logs) to investigate the opportunities for, and barriers to, learning that exist for employees in the four companies participating in our project. More detail of the methodological approach we adopted and the types and extent of our data collection are provided in the Method Appendix at the end of the book.

Given the data on apprentice learning emerging from three of our case studies and the perceived limitations of the situated learning perspective, we have developed a new conceptual framework within which to make sense of the barriers and opportunities to learning being experienced by apprentices in a range of company settings. This framework categorizes approaches to apprenticeship according to their *expansive* and *restrictive* features. In relation to the notion of "expansive," our use of the term is deliberate and has two purposes (Fuller and Unwin 2003a). First, we have argued that, from a definitional perspective (and, particularly, when it is deployed in juxtaposition with the term "restrictive"), the term "expansive" helps capture and illuminate an aspect of empirical reality found in our case studies. Second, as the research has progressed, we have been increasingly concerned to understand the interaction between institutional context, workplace learning environment and individual learning, and how differentiating between approaches taken to apprenticeship might provide a window on the wider culture of learning in the organization. Historically, apprenticeship has been conceived and experienced as a conservative institution with little or no opportunity for criticism, experimentation, or reflection (Engeström 1999). Given this, further work is needed to explore the extent to which contemporary apprenticeships that allow for more expansive practices can be aligned with the more progressive and transformational forms of work organization, production, and learning captured by Engeström's (1999, 2001) account of "expansive learning" and Wenger's (1998) "learning community."

Figure 2.1 lists the features we are associating with the poles of an expansive–restrictive continuum focusing on apprenticeship. Here, the main concern is to identify pedagogical features influencing the quality of apprentice learning.

| EXPANSIVE | RESTRICTIVE |
| --- | --- |
| Participation in multiple communities of practice inside and outside the workplace | Restricted participation in multiple communities of practice |
| Primary community of practice has shared "participative memory": Cultural inheritance of apprenticeship | Primary community of practice has little or no "participative memory": no or little tradition of apprenticeship |
| Breadth: Access to learning fostered by cross-company experiences built into programme | Narrow: Access to learning restricted in terms of tasks/knowledge/location |
| Access to range of qualifications including knowledge-based vocational qualifications | Access to competence-based qualifications only |
| Planned time off the job including for college attendance and for reflection | Virtually all on the job; limited opportunities for reflection |
| Gradual transition to full participation | Fast: Transition as quick as possible |
| Apprenticeship aim: Rounded expert/full participant | Apprenticeship aim: Partial expert/full participant |
| Post-apprenticeship vision: Progression for career | Post-apprenticeship vision; static for job |
| Explicit institutional recognition of, and support for, apprentice's status as learner | Ambivalent institutional recognition of, and support for, apprentice's status as learner |
| Apprenticeship is used as a vehicle for aligning the goals of developing the individual and organizational capability | Apprenticeship is used to tailor individual capability to organizational need |
| Apprenticeship design fosters opportunities to extend identity through boundary-crossing | Apprenticeship design limits opportunity to extend identity; little boundary-crossing experienced |
| Reification of apprenticeship highly developed (e.g., through documents, symbols, language, tools) and accessible to apprentices | Limited reification of apprenticeship, patchy access to reificatory aspects of practice |

*Figure 2.1* The expansive–restrictive continuum.

Before focusing directly on the expansive–restrictive continuum, it is necessary to indicate briefly how our use of the term "expansive" can be distinguished from the concept of "expansive learning." The purpose of Engeström's theory of expansive learning is to achieve substantial changes at the organizational level: "The object of expansive learning activity is the entire activity system in which the learners are engaged. Expansive learning activity produces culturally new patterns of activity. Expansive learning at work produces new forms of work activity" (Engeström 2001: 139).

Engeström has designed an intervention strategy, based on his concept of expansive learning, to help achieve organizational change. He has written in detail about the nature of the intervention (see Engeström 1999, 2001), which is conceived as a method (known as "the Change Laboratory") to be followed by work teams, initially with the help of a facilitator. Although, for Engeström, the purpose of expansive learning is organizational transformation, he has little directly to say about aspects of organizational context (for example, top-down strategic decisions on product markets, competitiveness, and people management) which influence organizational learning. He is extremely interested in how people learn, drawing on the Russian tradition of cultural-historical activity theory (see Vygotsky 1978, Leont'ev 1981), situated learning theory, and Bateson's (1972) concept of learning levels. However, Engeström tends to jump quickly from this concern to a preoccupation with organizational transformation. In this latter regard, he tends to read across from the type of (organizational) learning taking place to forms of work organization and activity.

In contrast to Engeström's concentration on organizational learning, the focus of our conceptualization of expansive–restrictive approaches to apprenticeship, and to creating and analyzing the nature of learning environments, is on *people* and *learning* (workforce development). The purpose here is to identify features of the environment or work situation that influence the extent to which the workplace as a whole creates opportunities for, or barriers to, learning. By identifying such features and analyzing them in terms of their expansive and restrictive characteristics, we provide a conceptual and analytical tool for evaluating the quality of learning environments and for analyzing an organization's approach to workforce development. We do not assume that identification of a restrictive approach will automatically lead organizations to reform along expansive lines. There may be a host of strategic and practical reasons for why organizations might (rightly in some cases) resist making such changes (see Keep 2002, Keep and Mayhew 1999).

Nor, moreover, do we assume that creating more expansive learning environments will automatically produce new forms of work activity or culturally new patterns of activity. However, evidence from our empirical research suggests that an expansive approach to workforce development is likely to increase the quantity and range of opportunities for participation and, therefore, for employee learning (Wenger 1998, Fuller and Unwin 2003a, Billett 2004). Our evidence also allows us to explore the idea that an expansive approach is more likely, than its restrictive counterpart, to promote synergies between personal and organizational development.

In relation to our use of the term "expansive," we would argue that from a definitional perspective, and particularly when it is deployed in juxtaposition with the term "restrictive," it helps capture and illuminate a dimension of empirical reality found in the data. The ability to contrast expansive with restrictive has helped us to focus attention on issues, such as access to forms of participation and work organization within communities of practice, which are underdeveloped by Lave and Wenger (1991) but which have significant influence on the quality of the learning environment. Moreover, as the research has progressed, we have been increasingly concerned to understand the relationship between organizational context, workplace learning environment, and individual learning, and to understand how differentiating between approaches to workforce development may shed light on the relationship between them. We have hypothesized elsewhere (Fuller and Unwin 2003a) that an expansive approach to apprenticeship is more likely to contribute to, or even be in reflexive relationship with, the sort of organizational learning and transformation which Engeström has termed "expansive learning." In this regard, we suggest that more research is needed to explore whether approaches to workforce development that allow employees more opportunities to engage in learning can be aligned with the more progressive and transformational forms of organizational learning highlighted by Engeström (1999, 2001, 2004).

In our research, Company A provides an example of an apprenticeship consisting of many expansive features whereas Company B's apprenticeship is illustrative of a much more restrictive learning model. On the other hand, Company C exhibited a mix of features and could therefore be located between Companies A and B on the continuum. For illustrative purposes in this chapter, we focus on the latter two cases. In Company A, apprenticeship participation lasts for four years and involves engagement in a wide variety of departments within the firm, attendance at college to pursue vocational qualifications, and the opportunity to take part in residential, outward-bound-style activities. The apprentices gain access to multiple communities of practice inside, outside, and near the firm and to the rich opportunities for learning that this system makes available. In contrast, Company B's apprentices are primarily involved in one community of practice that centers on the operation of steel-polishing machines and where they learn from engaging in the practices of the shopfloor with other more experienced employees. They become fully productive in around six months. The apprentices do not have the opportunity to study for knowledge-based vocational qualifications, which could provide the underpinning theories and concepts of their wider occupational field and also facilitate their subsequent progression to higher-level study.

In the contemporary economic and social context, the use of apprenticeship to attain a restricted skill base may be viewed as limiting the apprentice's opportunities for personal development and educational and vocational progression. Within the power structures of the conventional employment relationship, apprentices will have little influence over such choices and therefore the scope of their learning opportunities. The likelihood of the apprentice having a restrictive experience depends, at least in part, on whether workplaces have mapped the range of tasks and skills and have designed a structured program to generate opportunities to learn broadly as well as deeply. In companies that have not done this mapping, learning is much more ad hoc and haphazard and is more likely to be driven by organizational and commercial expedience. In such circumstances, the institutional status and legitimacy of the apprenticeship, as well as the lived reality of learning, is likely to be weak. Overall, we argue that an apprenticeship characterized by expansive attributes will create a stronger and richer learning environment than that comprising restrictive features. All employees would, in turn, benefit from and contribute to this expansive environment. The expansive quality of the apprenticeship experience in Company A is a product of as well as a contributor to a learning environment in which employees at all levels share their skills and knowledge and have access to learning opportunities within and beyond the workplace.

## BOX 2.1

### Example of expansive participation in (multiple) communities of practice

Company A has a well-established apprenticeship program that has been used to develop successive generations of skilled and qualified engineers and technicians. Many of the company's ex-apprentices have progressed to senior management positions. Participation takes place over time and in many internal communities of practice (through rotation around different departments). Apprentices attend college on a day-release basis where they pursue knowledge-based vocational qualifications that can also qualify them for entrance to higher education. Outward boundary-crossing also happens when apprentices take part in residential courses to develop team working skills and, through the company's apprentice association, they get involved in charity activities in the local community.

## BOX 2.2

### Example of restricted participation in communities of practice

In Company B, the vast majority of employees work on the shopfloor as semiskilled machine operators. The company offered its first apprenticeships two years ago, as a response to difficulties it was having in recruiting adults with relevant experience. The company currently employs two apprentices in (steel) production processes. The apprentices are primarily members of one community of practice which centers on the operation of steel-polishing machines in a shopfloor environment. They have learned from more experienced employees and have become full participants in under one year. Access to participation in communities of practice beyond the workplace is limited to attendance at a series (about ten) of off-the-job, half-day sessions on "steel industry awareness." The apprentices pursue standards-based NVQs at work with the help of their supervisor and a training provider who makes occasional visits to monitor their progress.

## The expansive–restrictive framework and workforce development

Central to the expansive–restrictive framework is a broader conceptualization of participation than that highlighted by Lave and Wenger (1991). The framework provides an umbrella under which diverse forms of participation or opportunities for learning can be considered. In particular, it foregrounds the relevance of both pedagogical and organizational factors to the creation of expansive or restrictive learning environments. In addition to the framework's use in analyzing approaches to apprenticeship, we have explored how the concepts of expansive and restrictive might point to indicators by which the quality of workforce development and workplace learning environments might be analyzed. In this regard, we have developed two further applications of the expansive–restrictive continuum. The first (see Figure 2.2 below) is relevant to analyzing organizational approaches to workforce development as a whole. The second (see Figure 3.2 on p. 61) seeks to list dimensions of organizational learning culture that play a key role in shaping the quality of learning environments. As Chapter 3 will show, examples from other projects in the Network indicate the adaptability of the expansive–restrictive framework and its usefulness as a basis from which to identify context-specific criteria. It follows from this, that the expansive–restrictive framework has the potential to increase understanding of the learning environments being created in very different sectoral and organizational contexts. We suggest that the illustrations show that the nature and "productiveness" of the workplace learning environment will largely depend on the extent to which they are underpinned by the principles of expansiveness or restrictiveness.

In addition, it is important to recognize that individuals participating in the same learning environment may experience that environment as more or less expansive or restrictive depending on personal factors such as their socioeconomic and educational background, attitudes to work and learning, and aspirations. The illustrations in Chapter 3 address the relevance of the expansive–restrictive model for experienced and professional workers such as school teachers, and for adults who are attempting to reenter the labour market after a "career break."

Lave and Wenger's (1991) original theorizing primarily addresses the ways in which newcomers learn to become full members of a community of practice. They pay much less attention to the learning of workers who are already full members. Two projects within the Network have focused primarily upon such people. Helen Rainbird and Anne

| EXPANSIVE | RESTRICTIVE |
|---|---|
| Participation in multiple communities of practice inside and outside the workplace | Restricted participation in multiple communities of practice |
| Primary community of practice has shared "participative memory": Cultural inheritance of workforce development | Primary community of practice has little or no "participative memory": no or little tradition of apprenticeship |
| Breadth: Access to learning fostered by cross-company experiences | Narrow: Access to learning restricted in terms of tasks/knowledge/location |
| Access to range of qualifications including knowledge-based vocational qualifications | Little or no access to qualifications |
| Planned time off the job, including for knowledge-based courses and for reflection | Virtually all on the job; limited opportunities for reflection |
| Gradual transition to full, rounded participation | Fast: Transition as quick as possible |
| Vision of workplace learning: Progression for career | Vision of workplace learning; static for job |
| Organizational recognition of, and support for, employees as learners | Lack of organizational recognition of, and support for, employees as learners |
| Workforce development is used as a vehicle for aligning the goals of developing the individual and organizational capability | Workforce development is used to tailor individual capability to organizational need |
| Workforce development fosters opportunities to extend identity through boundary-crossing | Workforce development limits opportunities to extend identity: Little boundary-crossing experienced |
| Reification of "workplace curriculum" highly developed (e.g., through documents, symbols, language, tools) and accessible to apprentices | Limited reification of "workplace curriculum" patchy access to reificatory aspects of practice |
| Widely distributed skills | Polarized distribution of skills |
| Technical skills valued | Technical skills taken for granted |

| | |
|---|---|
| Knowledge and skills of whole workforce developed and valued | Knowledge and skills of key workers/groups developed and valued |
| Team work valued | Rigid specialist roles |
| Cross-boundary communication encouraged | Bounded communication |
| Managers as facilitators of workforce and individual development | Managers as controllers of workforce and individual development |
| Chances to learn new skills/jobs | Barriers to learning new skills/jobs |
| Innovation important | Innovation not important |
| Multidimensional view of expertise | Unidimensional top-down view of expertise |

*Figure 2.2* Approaches to workforce development.

Munro examined the ways in which the learning opportunities of cleaners and careworkers were enabled or constrained by their working procedures and contexts. Heather Hodkinson and Phil Hodkinson have examined the workplace learning of secondary school teachers. When looking at the learning of these groups of different types of employees, it is important to make much more central some key issues that are, at best, marginalized in the Lave and Wenger account. These include

- the unequal and often contested nature of labour relations;
- issues of worker status (or lack of it);
- the extent to which workers are sometimes isolated from each other, rather than working closely in groups which might more readily be described as communities of practice.

Furthermore, in either case, the nature of the specific working practices, including what Wenger (1998: 83) terms a repertoire of "actions, discourses and tools," may or may not be conducive to effective learning. The expansive–restrictive framework is a useful device for analyzing the potential of a workplace for the learning of such experienced members of the workforce.

The expansive–restrictive framework enables us to expose the features of different learning environments and so make them available for inspection and critique. We suggest that there are two broad categories of expansive and restrictive features: Those which arise from understandings about the organizational context and culture (for example, work organization, job design, control, and distribution of knowledge and skills); and those which relate to understandings of how employees learn (through engaging in different forms of participation).

In focusing on the creation of learning environments, it is important to clarify the relationship between individuals and the opportunities and barriers to learning they may encounter at work. We agree with Billett (2004) that there is a distinction between the extent to which the organizational and pedagogical context affords access to diverse forms of participation and the extent to which individuals "elect to engage" in those opportunities, through the exercise of individual agency. The reasons why individuals engage and respond differently to the (same) workplace learning environment are explained by writers such as Hodkinson and Hodkinson (2004) in terms of individual biographies and dispositions for learning. Eraut et al., on the other hand, have a "pragmatic focus on knowledge use." They describe "personal knowledge" as, "what people bring to practical situations that enables them to think and perform. Such personal knowledge is acquired not only through the use of public knowledge but is also constructed from personal experience and reflection" (Eraut et al. 2000: 233).

While being in broad sympathy with Billett, Eraut, and Hodkinson and Hodkinson in valuing the individual perspective, we are wary of the dangers of excessive individualism or voluntarism. In this regard, we are guided by Marx's insight that: "Men make their own history, but they do not make it just as they please; they do not make it under circumstances chosen by themselves, but under circumstances directly encountered, given and transmitted from the past" (Marx cited in Armstrong 1987: 21).

Hence, in our view, an overemphasis on the structural character and environmental features of organizational context can underplay the role of individuals' backgrounds, prior attainments, attitudes, wider experiences, and agency, whereas an overemphasis on the individual can divert attention from the influence of the organizational and wider institutional context in which learning at work occurs. In order to clarify our position on this issue, we are developing the metaphor of "learning territory." By this, we mean that every individual has, and has had, access to a (unique) range of learning opportunities that make up their learning territory. The territory is divided into regions. For example, one region would cover classroom-based learning and qualifications, whilst another would cover learning at home. A key region for employees is the workplace. We argue that the character and scope of the individual's learning territory (as well as how they respond to it) influences how he or she perceives and engages with opportunities and barriers to learning at work. In terms of the focus of this chapter, we are interested in understanding the extent to which the creation of expansive learning environments can act as a mechanism for "smoothing" out individual differences and fostering more even take-up of opportunities and, by so doing, can facilitate the integration of personal and organizational development.

An important dimension of participation, and, therefore of unpacking expansive and restrictive approaches to workforce development, relates to the opportunity employees have to acquire expertise. We would argue that an expansive view of expertise entails the creation of environments that allow for substantial horizontal, cross-boundary activity, dialogue, and problem-solving. This fits with Engeström et al.'s (1995) review of expertise where they characterize the conventional vertical view of expertise as top-down. Here, knowledge resides in the experts who can (elect) to transfer it to "novices." Engeström and his colleagues acknowledge that this vertical dimension is important but argue that a "broader, multidimensional view of expertise" with an emphasis on the horizontal dimension is "rapidly becoming increasingly relevant for the understanding and acquisition of expertise" (Engeström et al. 1995: 319).

In terms of the expansive–restrictive framework, it follows that there is overlap and interrelation between the view of expertise adopted and existing organizational factors, such as the way work is organized and jobs are designed. In Figure 2.2, we located a "multidimensional" view of expertise at the expansive pole and a "unidimensional top-down" view of expertise at the restrictive pole. We would argue that in order to be consistent, an approach to workforce development that incorporates a multidimensional view of expertise should also adopt an expansive approach to work organization and job design. The following vignettes from our research are illustrative of how changes in job design and work organization can facilitate an expansive approach to the acquisition of expertise and, hence, foster workforce learning.

Several writers have stressed that the way in which work and jobs are designed directly affects the amount and type of knowledge available to and created and needed by employees (see, *inter alia*, Appelbaum and Batt 1994, Nonaka and Takeuchi 1995). The conceptualization of knowledge and work has been advanced by the work of the German researcher, Kruse (1986) who conceived the term *Arbeitsprozesswissen* (translated in English as "work-process knowledge"). Boreham builds on this work and explains:

**BOX 2.3**

### *Example of work organization, job design, and the acquisition of expertise*

Company C is a steel "stockholder" with some eighty employees. It is part of a large Swedish corporation but operates as a standalone business buying and selling steel. In order to compete, Company C must successfully market and sell its steel products by assuring their quality, value for money, and the efficiency of the company's services. To meet these business goals, the company is investing in management development and customer-service training.

To address the concern that sales staff had developed specialist knowledge of a limited number of products, the company decided to rearrange the way their work was organized, jobs were designed, and the way desks were arranged. Under the new system, sales staff were required to sell all the company's product lines, hence, they needed to learn about different products and get to know new customers. To support the change and to encourage the sharing of knowledge and information, desks were reconfigured in a circular seating arrangement ,which facilitated knowledge exchange and problem-solving.

Interviews indicated that while some of the sales staff had initially felt that their specialist (expert) status would be undermined by the changes, in practice they perceived that they had added to their knowledge and had gained from seeing how other people worked and the greater opportunities available for collaborative problem-solving.

**BOX 2.4**

### *Example of job design and the acquisition of expertise*

Company D employs some 300 people and manufactures large steel rods and bars, mainly for use in the construction industry. Management and unions have negotiated a substantial package of changes in employees' pay, terms, and conditions, involving a reorganization of shifts and shift patterns and the guarantee of pay rises for those workers signed off as competent in 60 percent or more of their shift's tasks. A simplified and less highly stratified division of labor was introduced to encourage flexible working and to reduce what were seen as restrictive practices. An important component of the new system related to the creation of a new post of team leader to replace the traditional job of foreman. Several of the team leaders had previously been foremen and were able to contrast the roles. There were two major extensions to the original job and both of these were direct consequences of the reorganization of work, pay, and conditions. First, team leaders were responsible for helping all members of their teams to achieve the 60 percent "competency threshold." In some cases, this meant that much of their time was spent training others and recording their achievements. Second, tasks relating to the organization of work and the attainment of targets (for example, on production, and health and safety) were delegated from shift managers to team leaders, so team leaders were now responsible for motivating their teams as well as monitoring progress. The extended job design together with support from off-the-job workshops created opportunities for new learning and a multidimensional approach to the acquisition of expertise.

The new idea which the concept of work process knowledge introduced is that workers need to understand not just the technical system they are operating, but the work process in which they themselves are participating—and creating—by way of operating that system. And this involves reconceptualizing the worker as a member of a much broader system, where knowledge is partly owned by the individual workers and partly by the organization.

(Boreham 2002: 10)

This emphasis on knowledge as being shared and mutually created across all parts of a workplace is particularly helpful to our understanding of where knowledge fits in terms of the expansive–restrictive continuum. Boreham (2002) acknowledges that many workplaces still operate along Fordist and Taylorist lines with strict boundaries between workers so that knowledge is seen as the preserve of those on higher grades. Huys and Hootegem (2002) stress that this conservatism is very powerful because traditional ways of working are particularly resilient despite many exhortations from external bodies, including governments, for change. In our case-study examples, a shift toward the expansive end of the continuum occurred when knowledge was seen to be a central component of all jobs and that employees needed to cross workplace boundaries in order to both demonstrate their existing knowledge and acquire new knowledge.

We have suggested that an important shortcoming of Lave and Wenger's (1991) situated-learning perspective was that it does not include a role for formal education institutions in the workplace entrant's learning process (see Fuller and Unwin 1998). Indeed, they see the off-the-job educational components in their case studies of naval quartermasters and butchers as adding little or having a detrimental effect. Young (2004) argues that the situated-learning perspective is based on a "social constructivist" view of knowledge. He suggests that a weakness in this approach is that it conceives *all* knowledge as situated or context-specific and fails to recognize that there are different types of knowledge, some of which are more situated than others.

In some of the cases we have been investigating, workplace learning includes off-the-job provision leading to qualifications. We would argue that the opportunity to study away from the workplace and to gain knowledge-based qualifications provides an expansive dimension to workforce development in that it: (a) gives employees the opportunity to extend their membership to other communityies of practice and to cross boundaries between communities of practice; (b) provides for employees to "stand back" from, and reflect on, workplace practice; and (c) provides the chance to pursue knowledge-based courses and qualifications. These three points recall the contrasting forms of participation available to apprentices in Companies A and B. In terms of courses and qualifications, Company A's apprentices have access to a range of qualifications, including knowledge-based awards pursued at college. This gives the participant access to theoretical and conceptual knowledge and understanding that is unlikely to be made available solely through experience on the job. It also offers the option of gaining the sort of general vocational and educational credential that qualifies recipients to enter higher-level education and that can support career progression.

The vignettes in Boxes 2.5 and 2.6 draw attention to the different types of knowledge and qualifications available in our case-study companies and to the implications for the learning experiences of employees.

**BOX 2.5**

*Example of work-based qualifications*

Company C, the steel stockholder, employs one business administration apprentice (John). The apprenticeship is entirely work based, and the apprentice is expected to learn his skills on the job and from more experienced colleagues. In Lave and Wenger's terms, John is clearly a legitimate peripheral participant engaged in a process of learning to become a full participant. He has access to the situated, context-specific knowledge available in the workplace necessary to becoming a "knowledgeable practitioner" in the community of practice. As part of his apprenticeship, John is working towards the competence-based NVQ in business administration, which assumes that all vocational knowledge is embedded within workplace performance. The apprentice is, therefore, denied the opportunity to acquire conceptual and theoretical knowledge, and knowledge-based qualifications. The latter become important if this young man wants to gain access to higher level courses of study. John's position is discussed in more detail in Chapter 3.

**BOX 2.6**

*Example of non-job-related, knowledge-based qualifications*

Company D has a tradition of supporting employees who want to take up educational opportunities outside work in their own time on the basis that it creates good will, helps the individual, and may promote employee loyalty. Individuals are invited to make requests to the Personnel Manager for financial help in paying course fees. Examples include four men, aged between thirty-nine and forty-four, who are studying as follows:

- to teach basic skills;
- for a humanities degree;

- for a Higher National Certificate in Business and Information Systems;
- for a computing and IT degree.

Although they recognize that there is no direct relationship between their work for the company and the topics they are studying, the men believe that the courses are helping them to maintain a positive attitude at work despite there being negligible possibilities for any career progression. They had all chosen knowledge-based courses to be stretched intellectually and because they led to well-respected qualifications which might be useful should they need to seek alternative employment.

## Summary

This chapter has provided a detailed introduction to a conceptual tool, referred to as the *expansive–restrictive* continuum, which the Network has used as a means of analyzing the differences between workplace learning environments. The continuum evolved from our research into the reasons why apprentices in the UK experience very different approaches to VET and to working life. Those differences arise out of a complex set of factors that determine the way in which one organisation will create and provide a different type of learning environment to another. The value of the expansive–restrictive continuum is that it can be used by organizations to analyze the extent to which they might be able to improve the quality of the learning environment for the whole workforce.

In the next chapter, the applications of the expansive–restrictive framework are explored in relation to the diverse sectors included across the Network's projects.

# Chapter 3

# Applying the expansive–restrictive framework

## Introduction

Participating in a network of projects provided the opportunity to consider the relevance of the expansive–restrictive framework to the sorts of learning environments created in contrasting sectors and organizational contexts and for employees at different levels. In Chapter 2 we saw how the framework could be applied to understanding contrasting approaches to apprenticeship and workforce development in the steel and metals sector. This chapter extends the analysis by indicating how the concept of an expansive–restrictive continuum facilitates greater understanding of the learning experiences of workers in a variety of sectors, workplace learning sites, and to individuals at various stages in their learning and working careers. Illustrations from each of the Network's projects are provided as subsections of the chapter.

## I Implications for individual progression

In this section, we provide examples of how the progression of individual participants in our case studies was affected by the extent to which their companies offered a more expansive or restrictive approach to workforce development.

### John

John is the apprentice in Company C (the steel stockholder), which, as we mentioned in Chapter 2, could be located neither at the expansive nor restrictive end of the continuum. John was advised by his external training provider to follow an apprenticeship in business administration

*Lead authors: Alison Fuller and Lorna Unwin*

as this provided a general framework for gaining competence in administrative activities through learning on the job. For several months, John was indeed able to gain experience in the administrative aspects of the business. However, his training and development were very loosely planned, with no off-the-job provision, and he had little opportunity to make formal progress toward the qualifications specified in his apprenticeship program. During a period in the quality-assurance department, John was pleased to be offered a permanent job there. John believed that he would have the chance to become fully skilled and integrated into this area of the company's practice. The downside was that he would not be able to move around other departments and, therefore, would have less access to learning in other communities of practice. At this point, John stopped seeing himself as an apprentice on the grounds that he now had "a proper job" and, because of this, a new status and identity. Within a few weeks of his appointment, however, John was moved to another part of the company, where he was required to process the routine paperwork generated by the warehouse and transport function of the business. In Lave and Wenger's (1991) terms, he had been uprooted from a trajectory where he was well on the way to full participation and relocated back to the periphery of a different department. Although it can be argued that, as a result of the change, he had access to a new community of practice and its learning opportunities, the fact that his newly established expectations had been dashed made it much more difficult for him to interpret the move positively and left him confused about his status in the company.

In John's case, there are potentially more possibilities for career and personal development as a wider range of activities are available within the company and, potentially, its parent company. As has already been mentioned, John has had the opportunity to work in different parts of the business although, we would add, his ambiguous status in the company has impinged on the quality (legitimacy) of his participation in the communities of practice in which he has worked. As an individual, John has the advantage of having attained A-level qualifications with grades high enough to enter university and having highly developed information-technology (IT) skills. He told us that if his opportunities continue to be limited at the company, he would look elsewhere for a job or, alternatively, apply to higher education. John has the background, ability, and self-esteem to envision himself in new situations and to embrace new identities—social and cultural capital that the two apprentices at the restrictive Company B do not seem to have.

### Sarah

One of the apprentices in our project provides another interesting illustration of the interaction of an individual's approach to workplace learning and the learning opportunities afforded by the company. Sarah has recently completed an apprenticeship in accountancy with Company A. She can be described as a highly focused, goal-oriented, and lively person. Sarah decided during her secondary education that she wanted to become a professional management accountant. She took and passed appropriate A levels, including mathematics, and researched the quickest route to achieving her goal. This showed that if she took up an apprenticeship leading to the Accountancy Technician Certificate she would be qualified to pursue a route to professional status. Consequently, she "self-selected" into the company as it offered her the opportunity to complete the apprenticeship as quickly as she was able, plus it provided financial support and time off to attain her professional qualifications via part-time study. At the time of writing, Sarah is well on her way to achieving professional status and at a younger age than would have been possible if she had first taken an accountancy degree. Sarah is very happy with the working and learning environment she is experiencing at the company, but she is very clear that if the opportunities she expected had failed to materialize she would have sought an alternative route to meeting her goals. Sarah is a young woman with clearly defined career and personal goals. So far, she is achieving these through the company's workforce-development strategy.

### Peter

Peter is in his early twenties and is also employed by Company A. Peter successfully completed his apprenticeship in August 2001 and was given a permanent job in the company's projects department. His current job title is "Ancillary Project Engineer." For the past few months, he has been working with five others on a project to redevelop one of the companies "power shower" models. Peter reports to the Project Team Leader with whom he undergoes a monthly performance review and development session. In addition, he has also been given sole responsibility for reclassifying the parts of the previous power-shower model as "old spares" and for moving these to a "spares cell." When showers are superseded by new versions, it is company policy to make spare parts available to customers for a period of ten years after the line has been discontinued.

Peter believes that his career progression in the company and in the wider labor market is linked to gaining increasing work experience and to proving his ability at this level, as well as to the attainment of further qualifications. Peter is currently considering which qualifications he should pursue in the upcoming academic year and to build on his apprenticeship achievements. He thinks it likely that he will take a Higher National Diploma (HND) in manufacturing, but he may decide to pursue management qualifications. The HND award is at the same level as his Higher National Certificate (HNC), Level 4, but requires him to pass a further four modules (the HNC required passes in ten modules). The company is willing to pay his HND course fees and will allow him to attend college for one day a week. However, Peter pointed out that he is expected to make up the time he spends at college by working longer hours on other days. There is no written agreement specifying what time he is allowed for study and what time he has to make up, but Peter says that there is an unwritten understanding that employees "make up their hours." Peter will talk over his options with the company's training officer who was responsible for him when he was an apprentice.

In terms of salary, Peter is now on a permanent-employee grade. Engineering apprentices at the company are paid a fixed salary but with an annual increment for the four years of the program. At the end of the program, apprentices who are offered permanent employment are transferred to a point on the normal company salary structure for the job they have taken.

John, Sarah, and Peter illustrate the very different ways in which young people experience the institution of apprenticeship in the contemporary workplace. Their pathways through their apprenticeships and beyond are closely entwined with the strategies, behaviors, and fortunes of the companies for whom they work. In addition, they, as individuals, monitor the extent to which their companies are providing them with the opportunities they desire in order to meet their personal goals.

## II  The workplace learning of secondary school teachers (Project 5)

The best and most effective teacher learning in Hodkinson and Hodkinson's study in secondary schools in England was fostered in expansive learning environments. Figure 3.1 sets out some of the main features of expansive and restrictive environments for teachers as

| EXPANSIVE | RESTRICTIVE |
|---|---|
| Close collaborative working with colleagues | Isolated, individualist working |
| Out-of-school educational opportunities, including opportunities to reflect and think differently | No out-of-school educational time to stand back, only narrow, short training programmes |
| An explicit focus on teacher learning, as a dimension of normal working practices | No explicit focus on teacher learning, except to meet crises or imposed initiatives |
| Supported opportunities for personal development that goes beyond school or government priorities | Teacher learning dominated by government and school agendas |
| Colleagues are mutually supportive in enhancing teacher learning | Colleagues obstruct or do not support each others' learning |
| Opportunities to engage with other working groups, inside and outside the school | Work restricted to "home" departmental teams, within one school |
| Opportunity to extend professional identity through boundary-crossing into other departments, school activities, and schools | The only opportunities for boundary-crossing come with a major change of job |
| Support for variations in ways of working and learning, for different teachers and departments | Standardized approaches to teaching and teacher learning are prescribed and imposed |
| Teachers use a wide range of learning approaches | Teachers use a narrow range of learning approaches |

*Figure 3.1* Expansive and restrictive learning environments for teachers.

identified in their research. The current organizational structures of English secondary schools, combined with an intrusive and dominating educational policy agenda, strongly frame the learning environment for teachers. There are both restrictive and expansive aspects to this. On the restrictive side, the isolated work of teachers, each in his or her own classroom, the extreme difficulties in getting time to work with teachers of other subject departments and with teachers from other schools, and the fragmented and externally driven nature of off-the-job training programs all restrict teacher learning. On the other hand, the pressure of changing curricula and other government initiatives triggers new learning, and teachers are privileged when compared, for example, to careworkers or cleaners, in that they do get some time for off-the-job learning, for example through staff-development days when pupils are not in school.

Given this broad and overarching framework governing teachers' working lives, Hodkinson and Hodkinson's research still showed significant differences between different subject departments in schools. Some departmental cultures provided more expansive learning opportunities than others, for example in relation to collaborative learning. Two departmental teams worked closely together, consciously learning off each other and continually striving to further improve their teaching. Also, in terms of the study, one of these departments stood out as unique in that the Head of Department saw his own learning and his fellow music teachers' learning as one of the explicit foci of departmental activity.

None of the teachers and departments in the study were at the extreme ends of the expansive–restrictive continuum, as represented in Figure 3.1. They tended to vary from criterion to criterion, so that even those closer to the restrictive end were still learning and teaching effectively. However, the evidence suggests that teacher learning could be further improved, if more effort was devoted to creating expansive learning environments.

### Development of the teaching workforce

Currently, the British Government is devoting significant policy attention and resources toward the further development of the teaching workforce. Hodkinson and Hodkinson's research suggests that at least some of the approaches adopted are likely to be counterproductive, as they press teacher learning toward the restrictive end of the spectrum. However, there are obvious problems about making the learning environment for teachers more expansive. Many of these problems arise from two sources. The first is the fact that, like other workplaces, (teacher) learning is not the prime objective of either government or schools. This means that desirable conditions for teacher learning often give way to more pressing organizational and policy needs. Second, the deeply entrenched culture of English secondary schools entails ways of working that tend to isolate teachers and also to separate out departmental cultures.

Despite these problems, there is much that could be done to construct more expansive learning environments, and actions could be taken at a variety of levels. The development of more expansive learning environments depends upon actions (and sometimes radical changes) by individual teachers, subject departments (or other working teams), schools, and national policy. Hodkinson and Hodkinson's work shows that each can make a significant difference, but the major gains will be made when several are working together in ways that are mutually supportive.

## The individual teacher

Many of the teachers in the study had done much to shift and maintain their own learning toward the expansive end of the spectrum. Many examples were found of dedication to personal and professional growth and development and to mutual support of colleagues. Others went further, looking to learn from students and, through foregrounding their own learning, helping to create supportive conditions for others. Most teachers can do these sorts of things, provided other aspects of the environment are favorable. However, much depends upon the status, career ambitions, identity, and self-perception of the teacher. These factors are also related to contextual issues such as home and family life, age and career stage, national and school structures of career progression, and salary, as well as the esteem of teachers in the wider community.

## The department

Subject departments can and should regard teacher learning as one of their explicit purposes, integrated into the continual improvement of their practices. Developing significant informal contacts, exchanges, and discussions, access to each other's lessons and work, and team-teaching and team-working to meet a specific problem or target are all potentially effective approaches. However, departments must balance the desirability for close collaborative working with the dispositions and preferences of some teachers to work more independently. Contrived or forced collegiality is likely to be counterproductive.

## The school

Schools should be able to move closer to a more expansive learning environment for their teachers if they plan for the development of such an environment and are prepared to support it. Opportunities for collaborative learning, boundary crossing, and involvement in work teams beyond the department could be improved in many cases. Physical and social structures and procedures can be developed to encourage teams of teachers to work closely together. Much of the current provision for teacher learning in England is tightly linked to the priorities of the Department for Education and Skills (DfES) and those of school policy. Whilst this may be important, there is also the need for space and support for learning that meets the interests and preferences of individuals, for example subject refresher courses. Staff-development days could be used flexibly to give teachers space to work on areas that matter to them, even sometimes being excused attendance in lieu of learning done in their own time. Long-term off-site learning is difficult to accommodate and needs imaginative support.

### National policy

There are a number of potentially radical policy changes that could have a major impact in terms of making the learning environment for teachers more expansive. Periods of paid educational leave would allow teachers to stand back and reassess their practice. There is also a need for policies that help schools enhance the learning that takes place through every-day working practice. Learning that is driven by targets and measured objectives can sometimes restrict possibilities, and there needs to be recognition and support for learning that does not fit these categories. An important feature of an expansive environment is the possibility of boundary-crossing. This is currently unusual in secondary school contexts. Many teachers would benefit from opportunities to work for short spells in schools and departments other than their own, which requires the development and funding of spare capacity.

## III  Relevance of the expansive–restrictive concept to adult reentrants

Evidence from Project 2 has shown that harnessing tacit skills in stimulating "expansive" learning environments sustains learning outcomes and facilitates the process of work reentry. Karen Evans and Natasha Kersh found that adults reentering the workplace after completing a college-based program may experience their working environments either as expansive (positive, facilitating further development, deployment of skills) or restrictive (negative, not facilitating further development).

The way employees experience expansive environments has to do with the feeling of "being a part of a team," whereas a restrictive environment is associated with "being an outsider or mere observer" in the workplace. Evidence from Evans and Kersh's interviews shows that employees experience their workplaces as either expansive or restrictive depending on the following factors:

- types of workplace environment: Stimulating versus dull;
- recognition of employees' skills and abilities;
- opportunities for workplace training and career development.

### *Stimulating versus nonstimulating workplace environment: Recognition of tacit skills*

The interview data from Project 2 shows that adults' perceptions of a restrictive workplace environment are usually associated with descriptions such as "boring," "nonchallenging," "repetitive," or "monotonous." The case of one woman's (Irene) work experience, for instance, provides an example of a boring or nonstimulating workplace environment. She works as an administrative assistant in a small company (powder-coating company). The way Irene describes her job clearly shows that she experiences her workplace environment as negative, not facilitating her professional development. She stresses that the nature of her job is very boring, and that there are not many opportunities to get involved in everyday activities:

> It's quiet, and I suppose business is not that brilliant, is it . . . , at the moment, I don't know, maybe, it's been a bit boring sometimes, shuffling papers to look busy. I feel like I'm just being paid to do nothing.

As a result, she is losing interest in her current job and wants to look for another job:

> It doesn't interest me at all. I'm very sorry. The product does not interest me, so maybe that's another reason as well. And, I don't know . . . I'm thinking, I probably shouldn't be doing all of this and should just go and get a job in a shop.

Marcia, who was an account manager in another small company, pointed out similar problems in her workplace environment: "When I first joined it was good, but because of the work relationships, the longer you're there, the more you become part of the furniture."

On the contrary, an expansive environment is usually associated with concepts such as "challenging," "interesting," "stimulating" or "motivational." An interview with Tracey, who works as an administrative assistant for the Metropolitan Police in London, shows an example of a stimulating workplace environment:

> I just think it's so interesting that I think I just get encouraged to go to work because of the interesting things that are happening around. There's a lovely atmosphere; there's a really nice atmosphere; I really thought people would look at you as if, like, they don't want you, but they didn't. The atmosphere's just great there, you know, and the work; I mean, obviously the other people who I work with have got their own jobs to do. Eventually, hopefully, when I have been there quite a time, I'm going to ask if I can be trained on another section of the police force. Get trained around the office, that's how I look at it. Quite a few people do that.

Diane, who works as a diversity officer, also speaks enthusiastically about her work environment. She stresses that her employers take on her initiatives, giving her a learning opportunity:

> It's fantastic; I couldn't have asked for a better chance, do you know, to do something positive. Diversity is a bit of a buzz word at the moment, and I didn't want it just to be just a buzz thing, to be politically correct. I wanted to do something constructive, something lasting, really create something for the members so that they feel, yes, this is working for us, it's supporting us, it's reflecting our needs . . . arranging meetings to go out and meet nurses and talk to them and find out what it is they want to see, what's lacking in their support system, so that if in any small way I can contribute to them feeling more valued, then that's great.

### Progression of career versus nonprogression

Evans and Kersh's data also show that employees evaluate their workplace environment by using criteria such as opportunities for career development and personal development. They experience their working environment as restrictive if there are no, or only very limited, opportunities for their professional development. In such cases, the interviewees stressed that they feel that their work is stagnant, and they are just performing their duties without any long-term benefits either for their companies or themselves. For example, take the case of Mark who works as a security driver for a security company. His duties include delivering cash and money to businesses and banks as well as collecting money. He is very pessimistic about his job and notes that there are very limited opportunities either for his professional development or for acquisition of new skills and abilities:

> I can't think that I am learning something. There is much I would want to learn but my managers would not give me a chance. It feels that every day is the same, like today is the same as yesterday, the same duties, the same people. I would want to undertake some further training, that's why decided to take the LU [London Underground] preemployment training program offered by one of the colleges of further education). With this job it would be the same for me for the rest of my life.

He feels that his tacit skills are not recognized and because of this he does not feel motivated to use or develop them. Conversely, an interview with Ahmet, who works as an overnight porter in a hotel, shows that he experiences his workplace environment as expansive, as it offers him opportunities for further learning and career development. He mentions that employees are able to undertake regular workplace training in health and safety as well as fire training. What is more, he has been offered one-to-one training by his manager in order to develop his computer skills as well as customer-service skills. The purpose of this training is to promote Ahmet to a position as a receptionist in this hotel. Ahmet is clearly enthusiastic about his workplace learning as well as about good prospects for his career development in the hotel. He notes that he is especially encouraged by the fact that his manager recognizes and values his personal or tacit skills such as communication skills, confidence, customer-care skills and foreign-language skills. All these factors motivate him toward further workplace learning.

Another interviewee, Tracey, also feels that her tacit skills are recognized by her employers, even if she does not have enough confidence to fully recognize those skills herself. Because her employers value her skills and want to promote her, there is a good potential for her to develop her confidence in the context of this expansive workplace environment.

## *Creating an expansive workplace environment*

The interviews confirm that employees may go further than simply experiencing their workplace environments either as expansive or restrictive. Evans and Kersh's evidence supports the view that they can actually facilitate their workplace being or becoming an expansive environment by taking initiative in various projects, enquiring about opportunities for their professional development and further training, learning from their colleagues, and so on. Conversely, employees who experience their workplace environment as restrictive often do nothing to try to change it to a more expansive one. Irene, for example, indicated that she felt indifferent about her job and not really interested in using or further developing her skills, thus contributing to elements of a restrictive environment.

# IV  Learning cultures and environments

The importance of creating an expansive workplace environment is clear. The examples from Project 2 show that individuals are able, to a certain extent, to create working environments that have some expansive features for them. Figure 3.2 below indicates some of the features that are illustrative of expansive and restrictive learning environments.

In this diagram, organizational characteristics that relate more directly to work organization (team-working, learning new skills/jobs, expanded job design) are highlighted. It is important to note that we do not underestimate the complexity, nor the contested nature, of some of these concepts. Some concepts can have ambiguous implications, depending very much on the context in which they are introduced. For example, multiskilling can be a mask for a move to greater work intensification and changes to contractual arrangements and payment systems. Helen Rainbird and Anne Munro have previously found that the same initiative (for example, job expansion) can be experienced by staff as either positive or negative depending on a range of factors, including staff wanting to know: Is it compulsory? Do they receive extra reward for extra tasks? Does it make work more interesting? Does it open up opportunities for job progression? (see Rainbird et al. 1999, Munro and Rainbird 2002.)

The complications discussed above can be illustrated through an example from the National Health Service (NHS). In the same department, there could be nursing auxiliaries (employed on national terms and conditions with enhanced payments for evening and weekend

Learning Culture/environment

| EXPANSIVE | RESTRICTIVE |
| --- | --- |
| Widely distributed skills | Polarized distribution of skills |
| Technical skills valued | Technical skills taken for granted |
| Knowledge and skills of whole workforce developed and valued | Knowledge and skills of key workers/groups developed and valued |
| Team-work valued | Rigid specialist roles |
| Crossdisciplinary groups/ communication encouraged | Bounded communication and work |
| Manager/supervisor as enabler | Manager as controller |
| Pursuit of formal qualifications valued/supported | Pursuit of formal qualifications not valued or supported/or seen as tangential to business need |
| Chances to learn new jobs/skills | Lack of workplace mobility |
| Expanded job design | Restricted job design |
| Bottom-up approach to innovation | Top-down approach to innovation |
| Formative approach to evaluation | Summative approach to evaluation |
| Individual progression encouraged; strong internal labour market | Weak internal labour market; recruitment usually from outside to meet skill needs |

*Figure 3.2* Learning culture/learning environment.

work) and healthcare assistants (on locally set terms and conditions with no enhanced payments), who do the same work and who may work alongside one another. In some trusts, if the nursing auxiliary completes an NVQ in care, she will have to transfer to local contracts, lose enhanced payments, and, therefore, see it as a negative development. On the other hand, the healthcare assistant working alongside her would have no contractual change and may see it as a positive opportunity for progression.

In the case of team-working, it might be better to talk of "working in teams" (that is, where information and knowledge are shared and there are opportunities to take on different tasks) rather than "team-working," which is often associated with increased work intensity. A number of developments such as team-working, task flexibility (multitasking or multiskilling) became more widespread with the growth of HRM and Japanization. Critics suggest that job enrichment is confused with job enlargement and that work intensification is overlooked (see Parker and Slaughter 1988).

The realities behind the terms used in Figure 3.2, above, are now illustrated using evidence from Munro and Rainbird's study of carework in two departments within one organization in Scotland.

### Carework learning environments

Munro and Rainbird studied two units within an NHS community trust, Clover Unit, a twelve-bed secure unit for clients with learning difficulties with offending behavior, and Arrow Unit, an eighteen-bed unit for clients with brain injury and challenging behavior. Both units have a relatively high client/staff ratio, because many clients require one-to-one care, and both have more professionally qualified staff than some sectors within the NHS due to the specialist nature of the care, though the majority of client contact is carried out by nonqualified care assistants. Both units faced similar problems related to a lack of funding for training and development for care staff and faced similar problems in terms of the lack of specifically relevant training in their particular fields. The NHS trust in which these two units are situated is committed to training and learning opportunities for all staff, encourages job progression, and works closely with the trade union UNISON to provide innovative learning opportunities for lower grade staff, such as Return to Learn.[1] The Trust is required to meet certain targets on the achievement of the Scottish Vocational Qualification (SVQ), Level 2, for care staff. The two units are based on the same site, within 100 yards of each other. Despite these similarities, the approach to learning and care-staff perceptions of opportunities for learning were very different.

---

1  The Return to Learn course, first developed by the Workers' Educational Association (WEA) in conjunction with Unison in 1989, was aimed at union members who had been disadvantaged in the formal education system and was designed around a combination of distance learning and small study groups. By 1998, 6,000 students had completed the program. It was successful in reaching nontraditional learners and achieving a dramatic impact on their lives (Kennedy 1995). From 1997 UNISON began running the program in partnership with employers (see Munro and Rainbird 2000), in which staff had paid time off from work to take part in the program.

### Clover Unit

Formal training here was limited to health and safety. Where a particular training need is identified, it is usually addressed within the unit by staff nurses developing a training session, for example on schizophrenia. No staff in the unit were taking SVQs or access to nursing courses, the Unit Manager had not heard of the Return to Learn program, and none of the staff were taking part in formal training outside the unit. The Manager saw the main problem of staff taking part in off-the-job training, as being the need to have staff on duty who are familiar with the particular clients and their specific needs. Therefore, using temporary "bank" (the internal NHS agency for temporary staff) staff was not regarded as a realistic choice.

### Arrow Unit

The approach here was very different. As well as the mandatory training, most staff went on control and restraint training, the Unit ran its own team-building sessions and periodically had staff "away days" as part of the development program. Six members of staff had progressed through to professional nurse training, either through the access to nursing program or through SVQs. Staff from the unit regularly take part in the Return to Learn program and complete SVQ Level 2. The Manager says that staff are actively encouraged to take part in *any* form of training and development. Few training opportunities are available during work time, but if a member of staff is involved in formal training or education, their hours of work are adjusted to accommodate the course. When a number of staff were completing their nurse training, the Manager had a copy of the college timetable and worked staff rotas around it.

Since a number of staff work extra hours on the bank and staff who have gone on to formal training continue to work on the bank, the Manager is always able to get temporary staff with experience of the particular unit and client needs. In this way, cover for training is not seen as a problem. In addition, the relatively high staffing levels in the unit are seen as providing opportunities for staff release. There are SVQ assessors within the unit, and there has been considerable effort to enhance the educational content of the SVQ, which has resulted in more positive feedback from the staff. Staff work in multidisciplinary teams, and care assistants are encouraged to work with greater autonomy than is usually the case. As part of a reassessment of practice within the unit, sixteen members of staff of all grades attended a three-day course on behavior (the new practice involves ignoring bad behavior and rewarding good behavior in contrast to the old practice in which bad behavior would normally result in greater attention). One careworker described how she was expected to share her experiences of the course with staff who could not attend and was given time during work to prepare for this.

### Comments

In this project, the expansive–restrictive continuum has helped to distinguish between the very different types of practice within these two departments. In Arrow Unit, a high value is put on the contribution of care staff and considerable attention given to their development. Staff work in multidisciplinary teams in which qualified staff are not seen as the only holders of expert knowledge and autonomous working is encouraged. Progression is actively encouraged and facilitated. In particular, the key role of the manager as enabler is highlighted in this case. In Arrow Unit, the manager provides encouragement, provides a flow of information about learning opportunities and, most importantly, ensures that the organization of work is used to expand rather than restrict learning opportunities even within the financial limits.

## V Expansive approach to education: Industry links

### The Teaching Company Scheme

Peter Senker's study of the TCS in Project 4 is a further illustration of the usefulness of the expansive–restrictive continuum. The achievement of TCS program objectives often requires extensive learning on the part of the company in which the program takes place. In some cases, the extent and nature of the learning necessary for program success is such that it requires significant increases in the expansiveness of the learning environment in the company. TCS programs are supported by an infrastructure that can facilitate this.

TCS operates through programs in which academics in universities join with companies to contribute to the implementation of strategies for technical or managerial change. Each partnership, called a TCS program, involves academic participation with company managers in the joint supervision and direction of the work of a graduate in a scientific, technological or management discipline. The graduates, known as TCS associates, are recruited by the academic department but are normally based full-time at the company. Associates also undertake supporting courses, covering both personal development and enhancing their skills where necessary.

The Scheme makes a grant toward the basic salaries of TCS associates and provides the academic department with the costs of senior assistants who take over a proportion of the normal workload of the academics so they can spend time at the company. Industrial and academic partners interested in setting up a program are advised by a TCS regional consultant. The consultant's role is to help prospective partners prepare formal applications to the Teaching Company Directorate (TCD) and to monitor approved programs. Once a program is approved by TCD, and TCS associates are recruited, participants are required to determine work schedules and to hold regular meetings of a local management committee (LMC) to review activities. The LMC comprises representatives of the academic and industrial partners with the TCD regional consultant.

TCS programs aim to help companies to achieve objectives such as:

- ensuring that products meet more stringent quality requirements, dictated by customer demand and regulation;
- developing new product ranges to meet the needs of changing markets, and developing and using the most suitable available technologies for that purpose;
- using more efficient methods for controlling production so as to increase the company's ability to meet the needs of its customers, for example by shortening lead-times;
- reducing work in progress and inventories and the costs involved in carrying them.

TCS programs take place mainly in SMEs. Often the learning environment is restrictive, perhaps because the company is run in a rather autocratic way by its original founder. For TCS programs to succeed in their objectives often necessarily involves the TCS associate playing a role in promoting a stronger, richer learning environment in the company. The associate is usually supported in this by the infrastructure of company and academic supervisors, consultants, and LMCs provided by TCS programs. However, the learning environment in a company is generally the consequence of strongly entrenched attitudes and practices, and it may be difficult to change it to the extent necessary to facilitate the innovations which TCS programs aim to secure.

In one company, for example, the workplace supervisor was very uncooperative at first. The TCS associate wrote reports, but the supervisor didn't read them. They were supposed to have a monthly meeting with the academic supervisor, but in the first five months, the company supervisor only came once. The LMC meeting takes place once a quarter, but the company supervisor came three-quarters of an hour late to the second one. The TCS consultant was not very happy. He threatened to pull the program as a way to make sure that the company supervisor became more involved, and this strategy worked. At the time of the research, the company supervisor was beginning to recognize the benefits of shared responsibility and delegation, and group participation and interaction have been encouraged. The result has been improvements in the open communication of ideas and proposals within the company. The TCS associate provided evidence that the company was not targeting its marketing efforts toward the most attractive markets, and changes in the company's marketing policy were made accordingly.

In a different company, ambitions for the TCS were very high. Previously, this company was primarily concerned with making its products more usable and economic to manufacture. During the past four years, it has wanted to base its designs on a deeper understanding of people. The TCS associate had the objective of helping to design products and services to provide a holistic experience. He has developed a process through which designers can move toward this new approach. At each stage, designers are presented with tools to allow them to go and find out how people live and to introduce them to people's experience. A director of the company was the associate's company supervisor in the first year. There are many engineers in the company who were skeptical about what he was doing, and the supervisor had to explain it to them.

The company's ambitions were, however, unrealistic. For example, the company wanted the TCS program to be a means of employing a data-mining specialist to develop and market data-mining services to client organizations. They needed to do this by convincing key decision-makers within client organizations of the value of what they had to offer. The company failed to make as much progress in this direction as it had hoped. The supervisor and the associate were in agreement that the program as a whole was not very successful either from the point of view of the associate's learning, or the company's interests, despite the associate's undoubted technical competence. The company failed to develop an appropriate marketing strategy. It attempted to market data-mining services to highly educated data analysts employed by large client organizations, but these analysts felt threatened by an outside organization which was perceived as trying to undermine their work. More recently, the company realized that it should have been marketing this service to commercial, nontechnical decision-makers within client companies. The company needed to do this by, as one interviewee said, "Being able to express what we've got to offer in very concise business-value terms." But the associate could not do this, "because she doesn't have the business expertise. And we've failed to do it because we don't understand enough about what she's doing technically."

The nature of the learning environment in an organization—the extent to which it is expansive or restrictive—is the result of attitudes and practices established over a long period. Accordingly, it may be very difficult to change. However, the examples given from interviews with TCS participants indicate that it may be possible to devise policies for improving learning environments through deliberate intervention, although the success of such interventions could never be guaranteed.

## VI Conclusion

In this chapter, we have used illustrations from across the Network to argue that the expansive–restrictive continuum is a helpful way of: (a) conceptualizing different approaches to individual career progression; (b) analyzing the character and quality of learning environments and cultures; and (c) identifying the opportunities and barriers to learning in a diverse range of organizational situations. Moreover, the framework facilitates analytical insight into aspects of the organization of work and learning, organizational culture and institutional factors that impinge on the lived reality of learning for a wide range of employees. In this regard, we would suggest that the approach shows both how the situated learning theory developed by Lave and Wenger (1991) can be built on as well as highlighting contextual issues, relevant to workplace teaching and learning, which fall outside their account. We would argue that the expansive–restrictive continuum produces a range of criteria that can be used to evaluate the quality of learning environments and against which recommendations can be made for improving learning support and practice. Finally, data from projects within the Network suggest that there may also be potential in applying it to sites in the public, private, and voluntary sectors.

# Chapter 4

# Learner biographies, workplace practices, and learning

## Introduction

In this chapter, we shift the focus toward the individual in the work context. We aim to show how aspects of employees' individual biographies as well as their prior experiences play an important part in facilitating the "interrelationships" between employees and their workplace environments. Workers' contributions to the *learning workplace* can be facilitated by such factors as employers' support and skills recognition as well as various elements of the expansive workplace environment such as opportunities for career development or additional on-the-job training. We conclude that learning opportunities and activities are more likely to be effective when they are responsive to the microconditions of specific working groups or contexts.

## Bringing the individual into social and organizational perspectives

Until relatively recently, most research and theorizing about learning has focused upon individuals as learners, within formal and nonformal educational settings. In contrast, for at least the past fifteen years, many studies of learning in the workplace have tended to emphasize an organizational or social viewpoint. There are at least two complementary reasons for this difference. First, it is important to understand workplaces as organizations where learning is not the primary activity. Consequently, the learning needs of individuals are rarely a high priority for any of the participants. Furthermore, most research on learning at work emphasizes the significance of everyday working practices or the regulatory frameworks that influence those working practices, and both of these can only be understood if an organizational stance is adopted.

*Lead authors: Karen Evans and Natasha Kersh*

For a combination of reasons, there is relatively little literature about learning at work which focuses on the role and significance of individual workers/learners. There is a need to build such individual worker/learner perspectives into the central social/organizational view of learning at work. The evidence from the Research Network enables us to do this.

Much recent research about learning in the workplace emphasizes participation. For example, many of the theoretical perspectives discussed in Chapter 1 stress the significance of belonging to communities of practice and of learning as a part of the process of becoming a full member of a community or a participant in an "activity system." These views of workplace learning prioritize the social dimensions of learning: The communal and the organizational. Learning is seen as a ubiquitous process, often subconsciously undertaken, for example though normal working practices. Conceptualizing the place of the individual within participatory studies of workplace learning that emphasize social processes is deceptively difficult. For from such a perspective, the separation between the person learning and the context in which they learn is artificial. Each learns in a context, rather, each person is a reciprocal part of the context, and vice versa.

There is a danger of exaggerating worker agency when we research individual actors situated in specific settings. This can be seen in some intervention studies into aspects of workplace learning (see, for example, West and Choueke 2003) that often highlight how major changes in perspective and work attitudes can be achieved with certain kinds of workplace intervention, but seldom consider these in the context of the prior learning and characteristics of the actors. Even fewer consider the structural conditions that fundamentally affect the longer term sustainability or transferability of these "interventions" into other contexts. In examining how workers respond to new work practices, discontinuities of change may be exaggerated ("participants became empowered and prepared to generate impressive solutions" [West and Choueke 2003: 224]) while the continuities of disadvantage are overlooked, and the question "How, and by what processes did this 'upskilling' or 'empowerment' reposition or reward people equally or differentially in terms of pay, power, prospects, influence, well-being or security in the short, medium or longer term?" is rarely considered. Social institutions, the institutions that so fundamentally influence our experiences in education and the labor market, continue to interlock in ways that shape life courses, yet these may be rendered invisible. We need to understand much better the reflexive ways in which people's lives are shaped, bounded, or change direction as they engage with education, labor market, and workplace organizations.

In our analysis, we see the individual and social structures as integrated, not separate. But people *are* separate from their place of work, as well as being integrated into it. This is because they have lives before, beyond, and outside their present workplace. They can and do step outside the workplace, but cannot somehow step outside social structures that are both a part of who they are and part of work and the workplace, as with all other human processes and situations. Workers are, thus, both part of and separate from the workplace community. We have argued that there is a need to further develop social and participatory perspectives on learning to accommodate this crucial conjunction.

There have been some attempts to focus upon these issues in relation to workplace learning, but each, in our view, is partial. Thus, Wenger (1998) is primarily concerned with the ways in which participation in communities of practice helps construct the identity of the learners concerned. On the other hand, Hodkinson and Bloomer (2002) focus upon the ways in which prior biography constructs dispositions that influence an individual's learning, while Evans (2002a) refers to bounded agency, a temporally embedded process in which past habits and routines are contextualized and future possibilities envisaged within the contingencies of the present moment. Billett et al. (2001a) examine the ways in which different workers react to the "affordances" for learning that the workplace offers. In Scandinavia, there is a tradition of life-history work in relation to workplace learning, which emphasizes the ways in which individual life histories of workers illuminate and represent deeper structural issues that interpenetrate their lives (for example, Salling Olesen 2001, Jorgenson and Warring 2002, Antikainen et al. 1996).

These and other studies have illuminated aspects of the problem, but each offers only a partial response. The analysis of the data from the projects that make up the Research Network has provided some ways forward. This analysis suggests that there are four overlapping and interlinked ways in which biography is relevant to learning at work. These are not separate in practice, or logically distinct. Rather, the four sets of learning process together express some of the complexity and multidimensional nature of the place of the individual in workplace learning.

- Workers/learners bring prior knowledge, understanding and skills with them that can contribute to their future work and learning.

- The dispositions toward work, career and learning influence the ways in which they construct and take advantage of opportunities for learning at work.
- The values and dispositions of individual workers contribute to the coproduction and reproduction of the communities of practice, organizational cultures, or activity systems where they work.
- Working and belonging to a workplace community contributes to the developing battery of dispositions and orientations and the sense of identity of the workers themselves.

In Chapters 4 and 5, findings from the research projects are related to each of these separately, followed by a concluding analysis in Chapter 5 about the relevance and significance of the four taken together.

## Bringing prior skills, understanding, and abilities into the workplace

Work performance has strong tacit dimensions. These implicit or hidden dimensions of knowledge and skill are key elements of "mastery," which experienced workers draw upon in everyday activities and expand in tackling new or unexpected situations. Previous research that focuses on tacit skills and their contribution to workplace learning has tended to focus on professional learning and work-process knowledge. Eraut, for example, has identified the ways in which the tacit or personal knowledge is necessary to convert codified knowledge into performance (Eraut 2000). From his perspective, new entrants to the workplace who enter with extended periods of training and high levels of codified knowledge need extended periods of supported practice to be able effectively to operationalize their knowledge in competent performance. Our work, by contrast, focuses on adults with interrupted careers whose prior experiences and tacit skills are often the most important resources they bring into tackling new situations. In the network project on Tacit Skills and Work Reentry (directed by Evans and Kersh), we set out to investigate the part played by tacit forms of personal competences in the education, training, and work reentry of adults with interrupted occupational biographies. Students were identified on a college course for adults aiming to return to work. Their experiences were followed through their course, in their job-seeking, and into the workplace. The research shows that adults are often able to use previously acquired personal competences in flexible and developmental ways as they move between roles and settings. Respondents highlighted the importance of such personal competences as time management, juggling different tasks or activities, handling routine work, prioritizing, and ability to communicate with other people. Acquired attributes such as determination and willingness to learn were also important. Other competences were more context specific.

Adults entering new working environments (analyzed as expansive–restrictive by Fuller and Unwin in Chapters 2 and 3), can under "expansive" conditions experience their work as a continuous engagement in acquiring new skills and deploying their prior skills in new circumstances. Workers can then use their past knowledge and skills to succeed at work and to build up new knowledge and new skills. Recognition and deployment of tacit skills in the workplace can facilitate these learning processes, together with the construction of further learning opportunities and outcomes, for the firm and for the individual worker. This "upward spiral" does not occur smoothly or simply. In some cases, transitions into new working environments will result in disjunction, drift, and stress. These are complex social processes. As shown in Chapters 2 and 3, the work environment is a crucial element in these processes.

In the research undertaken by Evans and Kersh (see also Evans et al. 2004a) on the learning and work transitions of adults, we have been able to illustrate how prior skills and knowledge relevant to particular occupations may be acquired very unconventionally, by presenting the case of Anna. Anna's job placement involved work at a social-service centre, assisting young people doing community work. She acquired such skills through voluntary work in which she helped mothers or fathers bring up small children, as well as through some difficult life experiences of her own:

> I think I've acquired, from my bad experiences [drug and alcohol problems, petty crime], that I've known the things that I wanted. I wanted to be listened to; I wanted to be heard; I wanted someone to take the time out to pay me some attention, or someone that I could trust. And I think it is the work that I do, they're the sort of things that are expected really . . . [I know] how to relate to them [young people].

She said that her young people thought that she was cool and she felt she was doing well. She was looking forward to becoming a support worker in social services. There is little attention to the relevance of such life experiences in the literature on career progression for young adults, yet these types of experiences and the skills and knowledge that stem from them are often crucially important.

Personal competences, the forms of skills and knowledge that have strong tacit dimensions, are of particular significance for workplace learning and movement between settings but often go unrecognized. Our research showed that naïve mappings of "key skills" between environments does not work. Trainers and employers may recognize the importance of tacit dimensions of skills and knowledge, but tend to see them more narrowly than learners. Attributes of creativity, sensitivity, and emotional intelligence often go unrecognized or are taken for granted (see Evans et al. 2004).

The research shows how individuals are able both to contribute to and learn from their workplace environments. Adults can contribute to continuous workplace development by utilizing and deploying their skills, which may be tacit. At the same time, various aspects of the workplace environment affect individual employees in ways that often contribute to their own progress and maturity. Such interactions between employees, on the one hand, and the workplace, on the other, take place in a process in which an individual employee becomes an essential part of the workplace environment. Even if employees are not particularly active within their workplaces, they cannot avoid being influenced by various workplace interactions and activities, for example:

- communicating with or learning from their colleagues and supervisors;
- taking part in various workplace customs and practices;
- acquiring new skills and abilities from their workplace experiences;
- deploying their own skills and abilities within their workplace environments;
- sharing their own experiences with their colleagues.

Furthermore, employees identify personally with their workplace environments if:

- they feel that they are contributing to the workplace environment;
- they feel that they are able to learn from their workplace.

Significant aspects of employees' individual biographies as well as their prior experiences play an important part in facilitating the "inter-relationships" between employees and their workplace environment. In other words, peoples' identities and dispositions as well as their social skills, including various social attributes such as "attitudes and norms of behavior" (Green 1999: 128) are significant parts of their workplace settings. All employees have different life experiences, such as occupational, educational, and family experiences. Their individual experiences and personal or tacit skills, as well as their dispositions and attitudes, make their methods and approaches to the job tasks *unique* within their workplace environments, yet there are broad "social regularities" that can also be identified. Our findings support the argument that recognition and self-recognition of tacit skills and personal competences could encourage learners to deploy and develop them further within a learning environment (see Box 4.1 and Evans et al. 2004a, Kersh and Evans 2005 for further information and cases).

---

### BOX 4.1

#### *Recognition of tacit skills*

Tacit forms of personal competences that are important for adults moving between roles and settings are related to attitudes and values, learning competences, social/cooperative competences, content-related and practical competences, methodological competences, and strategic (self-steering) competences. Learners with more continuous occupational biographies recorded higher levels of confidence in their personal competences at the outset of courses than those with substantial interruptions, except in cases whose recent work experiences had been poor.

Case analysis showed how adults' learning processes are negatively affected where recognition and deployment of tacit skills is low. Conversely, positive deployment and recognition of these skills sustains learning and contributes to learning outcomes. The starting point is *development of awareness* of learners' hidden abilities or tacit skills by tutors and students themselves. Modelling of individual learning processes provided insights into adults' experiences by making the part played by tacit skills visible. Tutors and supervisors employed different methods to make learners' tacit skills more explicit: Team-work, one-to-one tutorial help, giving new tasks and responsibilities. Individual approaches are needed in designing methods, taking into account experience, background and disposition, as well as learning environments and cultures.

By deploying their personal competences or tacit skills that were acquired from their previous (or current nonwork) experiences, individuals influence and contribute to "shaping" the culture of their workplace and learning environments.

## Skills acquired from previous experiences: Deploying tacit skills in the workplace to change or personalize the environment

The findings in Evans and Kersh's study (see also Evans et al. 2004b) suggest that employees' prior experiences and dispositions as well as their cultural backgrounds may influence or even shape and modify their workplace environments. Individuals tend, to a certain extent, to personalize their workplace environments, in some cases even without realizing that they are doing so. A number of the "women returners" who have recently entered new workplaces have explained how some of the skills and approaches they are using in their new jobs are similar to those they had been using in their prior experiences (for example, educational, family, or workplace). Some adults introduce at their workplaces certain traditions associated with their cultural backgrounds or previous experiences. The importance of utilizing personal skills and abilities at a workplace has also been stressed in the interview with Maria, who works as a part-time supervisor in a primary school. Her own family experience enabled her to develop a number of valuable skills that she is using successfully in her work. While deploying her skills at her workplace, she is trying to shape an environment for children that she describes as "homelike," similar to the one she is creating for her own children at home. She maintains that her own biography and life experiences as a mother help her to be aware of the possible challenges of her job as well as to better understand the needs and attitudes of children depending on their age group.

Starting a course in the college of further education and participating in a number of classroom activities initiated by her tutor made her realize how important these skills are. Maria claimed that she was able not only to deploy her personal skills but also to develop them further within her workplace environment:

> I've learned [how to cope with various situations] as well, and I know I'm stronger in that, more than before [when I stayed at home]. It's, for example [in the college], we [. . .] got little time to

do so [much], and at home, I do the same thing, but now I know I can also do more than I used to do before.

While doing her job, she is seeking to acquire and develop new skills that would enable her to provide better care for children. Such a positive attitude toward her work has encouraged her to undertake further training offered by her employer.

The interviews conducted within this project indicate that employees may often use their personal or tacit skills while they are trying to become accustomed to or adjust to their new workplaces. The case of Nick demonstrates how he uses his tacit interpersonal abilities, manifested in politeness, patience, and affability with customers, in order to conform to the basic workplace rules, regulations, and general settings. He works as a sales assistant in a big furniture shop, and his duties, among others, include dealing with the customers and, as he describes it, "making them feel quite comfortable." He maintains that in order to do his job well and be a part of the workplace environment, he has to employ a number of personal skills that one would need for customer care. He is positive that the skills that are useful for this type of work are personal and cannot be "just acquired" from regular on-the-job training.

The research carried out by Fuller and Unwin on apprenticeship in the steel industry has provided an illustration of how an employee's prior skills and abilities were known and encouraged by his employer, this time in relation to the worker's personal interests and longer-term development. Barry was a production worker in a steel mill. He was an outgoing and social character who often spoke about his out-of-work activities, including voluntary work as an adult literacy tutor. The personnel manager had some funds which he could use at his discretion to support employees wishing to undertake formal courses and qualifications in areas unrelated to their work. When Barry requested financial help to pursue a formal qualification as a basic skills tutor, the personnel manager readily agreed. In this case, then, the employee brought his prior skills and interests to the notice of his employer and was able to take advantage of the opportunity he was afforded to develop in an area separate to his job. As a result of his new qualifications, Barry was able to extend his involvement in teaching adult basic skills and was hoping to gain paid work, with a view to making a permanent career change.

A number of the teachers in Hodkinson and Hodkinson's qualitative study of teachers' workplace learning also revealed the importance of prior knowledge and skills brought to the workplace. However, the utilization of those prior skills was not always straightforward. Sam moved to a new school to take over running the history department. In the last few months in his previous school he had also run the department there. When he moved to the new school and department, he found it very difficult. He was in a situation where he did not know the people he was to work with and did not know the organizational systems of the school, but he wanted to introduce changes. He initially found very little direct help from colleagues in the new school except when things went wrong. He did, however, have the basic prior knowledge of running a department and basic prior knowledge of teaching history, which allowed him to make decisions within the new context about how he wanted things to go. He tried things out in the new situation and adapted them as and when necessary. It took him many months to become comfortable doing the new job. His experiences demonstrate some of the complexities entailed in using prior experiences in work. Sam could not simply transfer what he had learned in one school into the second one. However, much of that prior experience was of value. It was useful, but not sufficient.

Interviews with many research participants have confirmed that factors such as people's personalities, dispositions, and attitudes are significant aspects of workplace environments that affect the ways that employees perform their duties, handle difficult situations and conflicts, or adjust to their new workplaces. Different configurations of employees' work and life experiences make their attitudes and dispositions distinctive and often valuable within their workplace environments.

Our case studies also show that an emphasis on interpersonal skills and empathy can reinforce gender-based assumptions and expectations. The opportunity to deploy skills and knowledge gained in home and family settings is most readily identified by women moving into jobs that involve caring and interpersonal relationships, whether in health and social care or in "customer care." College-based courses can enable adult learners to use these kinds of personal competences in classroom and work settings, but the most effective courses use them in the learning process as a key to deepening and extending knowledge and skills and to unlock new capabilities.

## Deploying skills acquired as a result of college experiences

Those employees who undertake any kind of college training have also commented on the importance of skills acquired as a result of such training. For some of them, their college training has stimulated positive changes in their dispositions and personalities, and, consequently, facilitated their positive attitudes toward work and learning, enabling them to apply their newly acquired skills in their workplace settings. This is illustrated by the examples given in Box 4.2

---

### BOX 4.2

### *Deploying skills acquired as a result of college experiences: Cases of Sue, Emma, and Jane*

Sue, who works as an administrative assistant in a government department, maintains that skills she acquired as a result of her college training are extremely valuable in the context of her current employment.

> I learned about quality, and customer service, and what it means to provide a good service and knowing actually how to work at improving the service, and what good service means to a customer and quality. And the quality and approach to quality, all that sort of thing. Again, managing people, I learnt about how to work as a team, a team effort. I learnt about different types of, different stages within a team. [. . .] I learnt about different theories of teamwork and information, managing information.

Acquiring new skills from her college training has facilitated positive changes in her personality, enabling her to develop her confidence and self-assurance.

For adult learners, a strong focus on learning and career was also important. Emma, who has got a position as an administrative officer at a magistrate's court talked about the importance of the college training, stressing that undertaking a course in management studies enabled her to develop a number of valuable skills, both personal and professional. She successfully uses these skills in her new workplace environment and is hoping to develop them further through

---

learning opportunities at work. Utilizing her skills and competences and taking on new learning opportunities makes her perceive herself as a part of her workplace.

Jane, who works as a nurse, has also stressed the importance of her training:

> the other things like how to actually handle people, it's what I learned from my training because before I started [. . .] I'd be very shy, [. . .] shy is not the word to describe me, but I would be very uncomfortable to look after the person, [. . .] it's very private, you know, [. . .], but since this training I've gained more confidence in how to handle these people so I'm not uncomfortable doing it anymore.

A focused goal-oriented approach to learning was not confined to our cases of adult learners. One of the apprentices in Fuller and Unwin's project has a very focused approach toward her own learning, which was reflected in her attitude to learning and career (see Chapter 3). Sarah has recently completed a Modern Apprenticeship in accountancy with a company making bathroom showers. She presents as highly focused and goal-oriented. Sarah decided during her secondary education that she wanted to become a professional management accountant. She took and passed appropriate A levels including mathematics and researched the quickest route to achieving her goal. This showed that if she took up an apprenticeship leading to the Accountancy Technician Certificate she would be qualified to pursue a route to professional status. Consequently, she chose to work in this company as it offered her the opportunity to complete the apprenticeship as quickly as she was able, as well as further financial support and time off to attain all the qualifications necessary to achieve fully qualified professional status. At the time of writing, Sarah was well on her way to achieving these awards and at a younger age than would have been possible if she had first taken an accountancy degree.

Returning to the adult learners studied in the project carried out by Evans and Kersh, the case of Mary demonstrates the way she was able to operationalize her skills and competences acquired as a result of her college training within her workplace. Prior to taking the course for the Certificate for Women in Management offered by a college of further education, Mary worked as a deputy team leader in a mental-health group. She was happy with her position and considered herself to be a part of the company. However, taking the course in management made her realize her full potential as a prospective leader. She maintains that she acquired a lot of skills, both personal and professional, while undertaking this course. She stresses that the course, away from the day-to-day pressures of the job, also helped her to develop her so-called *soft outcomes*, such as those associated with increased self-assurance and greater confidence, and this facilitated further her skills in social interaction, teamwork, and management.

These newly acquired skills facilitated her career development as Mary was promoted to the position of team leader. Mary's case stresses the significance of experiences gained outside the workplace and their interplay with an individual's career and skills development within the workplace.

## External factors negatively affecting learners at their workplace

A number of external factors may negatively affect employees' development and progress at work. The problems of difficult financial or family circumstances have been linked to factors that may negatively affect employees' or learners' progress. The case of Tina demonstrated that her financial circumstances affected her practical training. Tina was assigned to undertake her practical job placement in the business centre of a college of further education in London. The college operates a business centre, which accepts six students who are undertaking a course in administration (NVQs, Level 1 and 2) in other colleges. Her supervisor commented that her attendance had been very poor because she could not afford to pay tube fares to travel to work every day:

> I think she had financial difficulties which affected her work. Somebody told me, she never told me herself, but I think that in order to kind of make ends meet she and her mother [. . .] her mother worked shiftwork and I think she might have waited until her mum got home so that she could use her mum's travel card to get into college.

Interviews with women research participants indicate that for some of them it is proving to be very difficult to undertake additional workplace or college training because of family commitments. The problem associated with high costs of childcare has been named as one of the main reasons that prevent women from assuming a more active role in various workplace activities, including taking on full-time positions. Another problem that has been named in this context is that of health. Some of our respondents had interruptions in their occupational or learning careers because of health problems. These setbacks were often hard to overcome.

The research carried out by Senker into the workplace learning of domiciliary-carer support workers in the Caretree organization revealed a number of examples where prior learning and experience were essential in the choice of specific work and carrying it out successfully. It is important that each worker has a set of attitudes, life experiences, and skills that enable her or him to relate to the needs of the family in whose home she or he works. Barbara started working with Caretree after retiring (early) as a children's community sister. She trained as a children's nurse between 1965 and 1968 and took general nursing qualifications later. She had occasionally trained Caretree staff, passing on some specific nursing skills. She wanted to work as a carer with children only, because that is what she had done all her life and knew about. Joan, on the other hand, had only ever worked with elderly people. She was confident with them as she has learned how to cope with them over the years. She felt that caring for children would be too much of a responsibility. One worker, Denise, was willing to work with a wider range of clients. This reflected her own home background where she had cared for many years for her elderly mother, but also had a child, now adult, with Asperger's syndrome. In the cases of these individuals, their current approaches to working practice show some clear links to prior experiences.

There are important similarities in the use of prior skills by adults with continuous professional careers and by those of adults with interrupted occupational biographies. For neither group does moving into new workplaces involve simple transfer of prior skills and knowledge. Our findings resonate with those of Lobato (2003) in showing the importance of the actor/learner's perspective:

- The influence of prior activity on current activity and the different ways in which actors may construe situations as being "similar."
- What experts consider to be only a "surface feature" of a work task or problem may be structurally important for a participant.
- The multiple processes involved include attunement to affordances and constraints in the work environment.

- "Transfer" is distributed across mental, material, social, and cultural planes.

Skills and knowledge have to be developed and possibly changed as they are operationalized in the culture of new workplaces. Furthermore, it is not the skills and knowledge that develop, but the whole person, as he or she adjusts, with greater or lesser success, to working in a new environment. That adjustment depends as much upon the restrictive or expansive nature of the new workplace, as upon the prior experiences that workers bring. Put differently, the processes entailed can be significantly helped or hindered by the actions and dispositions of employers and coworkers. They are also influenced by the dispositions of the workers who are moving, as the next section makes clear.

## The significance of dispositions in relation to workplace learning opportunities

In the diversity of workplaces we have researched, our findings have shown that the way the learners perceive and respond to the learning opportunities within their workplaces is strongly influenced by their individual attitudes and dispositions. Learners bring to their workplaces not only their prior skills and competences but also their individual dispositions and attitudes toward learning. Learners' previous and parallel life experiences, such as social and educational backgrounds, financial situation, family life, or prior workplace practices influence and shape their outlooks and dispositions, which they bring into their new workplace environments. The workplaces themselves offer different opportunities for learning, and those opportunities differ for different workers, even in the same workplace. The differences in opportunity depend upon the way in which work is organized in any particular firm, and upon the position and job description that a worker holds. Thus, Rainbird et al. (2005) have shown that learning opportunities for cleaners and careworkers are related, amongst other things, to the relatively low status of the predominantly female, working-class and, often, ethnic-minority workers concerned. There are also significant differences, depending upon the different ways in which cleaning, social care in residential homes, domiciliary social care, and carer support are organized.

Our concern here is to uncover how different people respond and react to these opportunities. We have shown, in previous accounts (see Hodkinson et al. 2004) how Michael and Tom brought different dispositions to their work-related learning in the shared environment of the transport company for which both worked. Michael's long-term career with the same employer indicates acceptance and recognition of his skills within the work environment. Exposure of basic skills difficulties represents a threat to him, and, therefore, he avoids training or learning opportunities that take him out of his work environment. Tom works within the same structures, but his disposition toward learning leads him to seek out opportunities to strengthen the skills he feels he lacks, in overt ways and in new environments. The examples given in Box 4.3 demonstrate how individual dispositions affect learners' attitudes within similar kinds of workplace environments.

---

## BOX 4.3

### *Individual dispositions and learners' attitudes: Cases of Pamela and Maria*

Pamela and Maria, who both work in similar workplace environments (big chain food superstores), demonstrated different ways in which their individual attitudes and dispositions affected their workplace experiences, career development, and skills acquisition. In both cases, they are pleased to undertake additional workplace training offered by their employers. They find this kind of training very useful for both their present and future workplace and career development. Although both Maria (checkout controller) and Pamela (stock controller) are taking on these training opportunities, their attitudes are different; their individual dispositions influence their perception of their duties and responsibilities as well as their involvement and independence within their workplace environments. Not only is Maria enthusiastic about her workplace training, she also is continually looking for more opportunities to undertake relevant on-the-job training in order "to do a better job." For example, because she often deals with elderly customers, she is going to undertake in-service training in age-related sales, which she feels will be extremely useful for anyone communicating with elderly people. She has taken her own initiative and found out about opportunities to take on this training at her workplace.

Conversely, Pamela's attitude towards workplace learning opportunities is that of acceptance rather than of enthusiasm. She is happy enough to take on in-service training opportunities offered to her by her employers, because it gives her confidence in what she is doing during her working day. She likes her job, but she is not prepared to take her own initiative and to develop additional skills that would be useful within her workplace. Pamela is not active enough to enquire about further on-the-job training opportunities, as she is content with her job as it is. In this sense, her attitude toward her duties is different to that of Maria who is continually seeking to develop her skills.

The research of school teachers' learning carried out by Hodkinson and Hodkinson also showed how disposition and environment interact, by comparing cases of teachers working in shared environments. Malcolm and Steve were both male, white, middle-class teachers, in mid-career, working in the same English secondary school. At the time of the research, Malcolm had had three recent career setbacks, described in Hodkinson and Hodkinson (in press). Partly as a result of this, he was cynical about a new performance-management initiative in the school. For him, rather than an opportunity to organize his learning and development, this scheme was an unwanted intrusion upon his time and a further mechanism through which "Management" and the Government were trying to control his work and limit his professionalism. Steve was a Head of Department. He was enthusiastic about his work and had a deep commitment to his own learning. He usually found ways of creating learning opportunities out of anything he had to do. Consequently, he was initially enthusiastic about the opportunities that the performance-management scheme would bring. As the scheme progressed, he became rather less enthusiastic, because he found the input of his designated line manager unhelpful.

The three teachers in the art department (Hodkinson and Hodkinson 2003) shared a long-established communal disposition toward working, and their routine practices centered upon the shared ongoing development of new ways to teach art. Other teachers in the study were unhappy about such intensive collaborative learning. Such teachers learned through their practice as teachers, but their more individualistic dispositions limited possible collaborative learning opportunities. The examples given in Box 4.4 illustrate how the dispositions of workers interacted with each other.

---

**BOX 4.4**

**The dispositions of workers interacting with each other: Cases of teachers in the History Department**

Teachers in the History Department were divided over issues of collaborative working. Sam, the new Head of Department, wanted to encourage it, and two other teachers, Jasmin and Pat, were broadly sympathetic. Other teachers, including Malcolm, and Rachel—who arrived part-way through the fieldwork and effectively replaced Pat—preferred to work predominantly alone. Sam was frustrated in his attempts to establish more communal working/ learning practices and put emphasis instead on an alternative philosophy in which he valued his staff being able to work and develop in their own individual ways. Generally, the team was happy with this more laissez-faire standpoint. At the same time, as we have seen in the previous section, the organizational structures of the school meant that Sam had had little opportunity to develop collaborative approaches to his own job as a middle manager. In his case, the external dimensions of his horizons for learning dominated some of his subjective dispositions, unlike the situation for the art teachers and for Steve, where subjective dispositions and external structures were more synchronous.

---

Through these and other cases, the research has shown that dispositions and attitudes of individual workers may play an important part in facilitating the learning environment within the workplace. Interview data have indicated that a learning workplace is *co-constructed*, involving the following:

- intermediary support provided by employers/managers/supervisors.
- elements of the expansive (stimulating) workplace environment;
- individual workers' roles, initiative and involvement;
- employers' support, involvement, and awareness of their employees' dispositions.

Our findings support the argument that employers' support and encouragement could facilitate employees' positive attitudes toward work, career, and learning, and could influence the ways in which they understand and take advantage of opportunities for learning at work. By taking into account their employees' previous/current experiences and their dispositions as well as their cultural and educational backgrounds, employers can facilitate their employees' motivation and attitudes toward work and learning.

Our research indicates that some employers would look for generic or transferable skills in prospective employees right from the job interview. One employer, working in the area of social work, stresses the importance of skills such as "good communication skills, listening, giving feedback, building good relationships with the clients [. . .], being able to organize things, etc." Such skills in employees would contribute to the development of both a friendly and well-organized workplace environment. The employer notes that she always takes into account prospective employees' dispositions and personalities when employing people who intend to work with those experiencing various kinds of mental disorders:

> when I meet someone usually I can tell from their [. . .] personality, [whether they are] sensitive, caring, [. . .] understanding [. . .] nonjudgmental, sensitive to things like equal opportunities and issues around race, gender, people's culture. They need to be aware of those kinds of issues. If people are aware of those, they need to be aware of the impact of mental illness in people's lives. And not be judgmental. You can tell if someone is coming across if they're being judgmental and then that isn't what we're looking for. We need people who can be quite accepting and show acceptance and tolerance, who can be quite encouraging, who are themselves quite motivated because if they come across as quite motivated, then I know they're going to pass that on into the work they're doing. That's going to come through in their work.

Our interviews with a number of employees have shown that the issue of recognition of personal (often tacit) skills and competences is one of the most important factors that facilitate their motivation to use and deploy them within their workplace environments. If the employees believe that their skills are appreciated by their supervisors and colleagues, they feel more confident about making them visible through deploying them in a variety of activities. Taking into account employees' dispositions, identities, and backgrounds seems to be of importance in this context, as those factors may affect their motivation and readiness to deploy and develop their personal (tacit) skills. If employers are aware of such issues and take their employees' dispositions into account, this may help them to tackle more efficiently various problems faced by their employees, such as lack of confidence or feelings of uneasiness at work. In this context, the workplace environment could contribute to "shaping" or changing their employees' dispositions through a number of approaches that could facilitate people's confidence and self-assurance:

> Well, I'd have to find out in which area they feel low; I'd have to try and understand what basically they're not confident in and to see how they can practice and develop the skills. For me, when someone says they've not got confidence [. . .] I think [. . .] the only way you get that is by doing whatever it is you don't feel confident about and doing it over and over.

Employers' support and recognition of skills are significant factors that may facilitate production and reproduction of expansive and stimulating learning cultures (or environments) at work. However, the extent of employers' support and involvement may vary from workplace to workplace. Our research has shown that, in some cases, employees' personalities and dispositions enable them to contribute to a "stimulating or *expansive* learning environment or culture" for themselves, even without active support from their employers or supervisors.

## Individual workers' dispositions in facilitating the workplace environment

Employees can contribute to the development of a workplace environment which is *expansive* for them by taking initiative in matters such as inquiring about opportunities for their further training or career development, sharing their experiences with their colleagues, contributing to the planning and conducting of various workplace activities (Evans et al. 2004). The examples below demonstrate the ways in which individual employees are able and willing to create stimulating and expansive learning cultures at work for both themselves and for others.

The case of Mary, introduced earlier in this chapter, provides an example of a worker facilitating the learning culture at work initially for herself and later for other employees. Mary is a working mother with three children. At the time of the initial interview she had the experience of working as a deputy team leader in a mental-health group for four years. Mary worked on various projects to help people with mental health to socialize and to be integrated back into the community. Her duties and responsibilities involved supervising staff and managing various workplace activities, for example staff cooperation and communication with the clients.

The fact that she was able to deploy successfully her tacit skills in her workplace environment and that her skills were recognized by her employer facilitated her perception of the workplace as a stimulating and expansive learning environment where she could apply and develop further both her professional and personal skills. Working in such an environment facilitated further her attitudes toward learning. Mary is convinced that the success of the workplace could be facilitated by people's own initiatives and involvement. This is illustrated in Box 4.5.

---

**BOX 4.5**

***Facilitating the learning culture at work: The case of Mary***

Mary felt that she needed to develop her management skills as that would enable her to facilitate a learning culture for both herself and the other members of her team:

> I'm thinking that I want to retrain, develop my skills, develop my qualifications and be able to move on [. . .] I work quite a lot with people [. . .] I decided to develop my management skills, [. . .] in order to compete later on, or to provide better support for my team.

She took her own initiative and approached her employers with her thoughts, and, as result, her company gave her a chance to undertake a course "Certificate for Women in Management" offered by a college of further education. After completing this program, with her newly acquired skills combined with her positive learning attitudes, she has been able to contribute further to developing the learning culture at her workplace by actively employing her skills at the workplace, learning from this experience, and sharing her experience with her colleagues. Her confidence and self-assurance improved greatly as a result of various learning and workplace

---

initiatives and this enabled her to apply for the position of Team Leader in the same company when the post became vacant.

Her new position opened many exciting opportunities for her to contribute to shaping an expansive and stimulating learning culture at her workplace. One of her proposals involved launching an initiative to collaborate with the agencies or companies that deal with issues similar to those of her company. She believes that sharing experience and learning from each other provides valuable learning opportunities for herself and members of her team.

The influence of workers' dispositions and attitudes on the learning environment at work is also demonstrated by the cases of Helen and Anita. Both work as part-time careworkers for different care agencies. As careworkers, they are used to working on their own most of the time. Because of such workplace conditions, they both maintain that their personalities play an important part at their workplaces. Both Helen and Anita feel that their workplace environments do not provide many explicit opportunities for further learning and skills development. However, they claim that they themselves can actually contribute to facilitating learning while they work. Aspects of their individual biographies as well as their dispositions influence their attitudes to their duties and help them to facilitate learning at work. Helen, for example, thinks that she could learn a lot from her own experience at work. She utilizes her previously acquired tacit skills and develops them further as she is taking on her duties as a careworker:

> I can work with all sorts of people. I get difficult clients, [. . .] I have to work around that. And it tests my patience as well, you know, [. . .] it just helps me to stay calm and just think I'm going to come across a lot of stuff like this.

Anita, who works as a part-time careworker, is also taking a university course in nursing and social care. In her case, she is attempting to transform her workplace into a positive learning environment by deploying and further developing her professional and personal skills acquired as a result of her university studies. She thinks that her studies to become a professional nurse enable her contribute better to her workplace environment.

Anita's and Helen's cases demonstrate that workers' personalities, dispositions, and attitudes play an important part in facilitating learning cultures, even at workplaces where employees do not have many opportunities to learn from their colleagues or to take part in additional workplace training.

These examples demonstrated that the dispositions and attitudes of individual workers could be crucial in facilitating (or nonfacilitating) the workplace learning environment. The extent to which they are able or willing to contribute to the production/facilitation of learning cultures at work may vary depending on the workers' attitudes, dispositions, or aspirations as well as on aspects of their individual biographies, cultural backgrounds, previous or parallel educational or workplace experiences, and family situation. In addition, the employees' contributions to the *learning workplace* can also be facilitated by such factors as employers' support and skills recognition as well as various elements of the expansive workplace environment, for example, opportunities for career development or additional on-the-job training.

As with other possible learning opportunities at work, whether qualifications act as "enablers" of further development depends on the partly preestablished dispositions of the person concerned. Where the qualification is neither a means to an end which is wanted and recognized as valuable to the learner, nor experienced as important in developing wider personal competences, engagement in the learning is low, as shown by the domiciliary workers in the project carried out by Senker where some forms of learning are currently tied to the requirement to achieve compulsory qualifications. They will be required to take NVQs because of government policy for all careworkers.

The qualification is not well adapted to Caretree workers' specialized roles. It covers many tasks that these workers will never be required to carry out, for example tasks associated with work in residential homes. At the same time, it requires only basic levels in skills in areas where they already have far greater expertise. NVQs are improved continuously, and some, but by no means all, of the deficiencies identified by our research have been addressed since it was completed. Differing experiences and dispositions result in widely varied reactions to the work and learning entailed in acquiring this qualification. Several of the interviewees were reluctant to work toward achieving NVQs. See Box 4.6, which demonstrates the cases of Barbara and Denise.

In all these and other cases, the possibilities for learning at work depended upon the interrelationship between individual worker dispositions and the affordances of the workplace, rather than upon

---

**BOX 4.6**

*Interrelationship between individual worker dispositions and the affordances of the workplace: Cases of Barbara and Denise*

Barbara already had nursing qualifications and was not interested in doing the NVQ. Joan was doing it, but as a form-filling activity:

> It is like filling in a tax form. It is verbose. It is a waste of time and energy. It has to be done as a requirement. NVQs are not training. It's like going to the dentist, something you've got to get through. You've got to grit your teeth and do it. Some of it is irrelevant to lone workers. [. . .] Caretree work ranges from sitting, to being a companion, to nursing. The standards are written for people without any social graces. They are a waste of time, a waste of energy and a waste of money.

Denise on the other hand, was keen to do the qualification. She was worried that she could be considered too old to do it, especially as it is expensive for the company to assess and because she was worried about returning to written assessments. Her greater interest in the qualification may be partly because of the wider scope of her caring activities, which mean that more of the NVQ is of relevance to her.

---

either, taken in isolation. Horizons for learning are both subjective and objective.

## Employees and environments: Reciprocal relationships

In this chapter, we have considered various examples that have shown the ways in which employees' prior skills and knowledge, dispositions, and personal backgrounds may affect their attitudes toward work and learning, contribute to their success in their workplace and facilitate their participation in various workplace activities and tasks. Employees' personal and educational backgrounds as well as skills they have learned from a variety of experiences influence the ways in which they carry out their duties and responsibilities, deal with various workplace situations, make decisions, or solve problems. All employees bring their prior skills and understanding to their workplaces, and this affects the ways they perceive and perform their duties and responsibilities.

Employers' support and recognition of their staff's skills and competences are important factors that may facilitate their employees' confidence and self-assurance as well as their attitudes toward further training, skills deployment, and acquisition. If the employees believe that their skills and competences as well as their individual backgrounds are recognized, they feel motivated both to contribute to and to learn from their workplace environment. This can encourage continuous positive interactions between employees and their workplace environments where employees' dispositions and personal backgrounds contribute to the shaping and reshaping of their workplace environments. At the same time, while taking on their duties and responsibilities as well as participating in workplace training, employees may undergo some changes in their dispositions, personalities, and attitudes. Although employers' support could be an important factor in this context, the research has shown that employees' personal initiative can enable them to create a microculture of learning at work, even without their employers' active support and involvement.

Our findings suggest that a stimulating and expansive learning environment or a learning culture at work allows the employees to perceive themselves as part of their workplace, encouraging them to take advantage of further opportunities for learning at work. At the same time, all employees have lives outside of their workplace environments, and this broadens their outlook and gives them many (or at least some) opportunities to acquire and develop a number of additional skills in an "outside-of-work" environment. Various configurations of their everyday lives and experiences (for example, family, education, or travel) facilitate the development of their personal skills and competences that potentially may be used for the benefit of their workplaces.

There are two particular pitfalls for those wishing to understand workplace learning and for those wishing to influence and improve its practice. These are either to overemphasize individual agency or to slip into organizational or cultural determinism. The first can happen if an overrationalized and technical view of individual workplace learning is adopted. This is exemplified in some approaches to learning through individual choice or learning plans. Such approaches risk seeing the individual learner, perhaps working in conjunction with a mentor or line manager, as the prime determinant of learning.

In the ubiquitous audit culture, there is an understandable tendency to see workplace learning as the controled acquisition of predetermined skills, knowledge, and working practices. Someone (for example a manager, or government policymaker) decides what learning should be done, how the success of such learning can be measured, and how it will be developed. The risk with such approaches is the assumption of predictability about the impact of pedagogical interventions, across all relevant workers, in any targeted context.

Here we argue for a different approach. Within such an approach, the positions and dispositions of workers should be taken seriously, for example by providing some of the learning opportunities which they value, rather than those which managers assume they either need or should want. This means that much planning and activity should be responsive to the microconditions of specific working groups or contexts, as well as more macro-influences. To be successful, any approach will need to pay attention to power differentials and workplace inequalities as well as individual wants or needs. In short, the approach should be to encourage and facilitate learning through work, not directly impose it.

## Conclusion

In this chapter, we have argued that the relationships between individual workers/learners and workplace and organizational practices and cultures are complex and significant. Such learners are simultaneously part of the workplaces they inhabit and separate from them. We have shown some of this complexity by looking at overlapping types of interaction between individual and workplace context: How prior skills and experiences are brought into the workplace; how individuals differ in their perceptions and take-up of opportunities afforded by the workplace; and how employees can "co-construct" workplace opportunities and practices that influence learning by their attitudes and actions in the workplace.

Workplace environments are as important as training methods and supervisory skills in capturing and developing adults' skills, including their tacit skills. Labor-market training agencies, employers, and trade unions need to be better informed about the importance of employee dispositions and tacit skills, and the human resources which remain untapped when they are neglected. Examples from Network projects have illustrated these interactions between individuals and workplace contexts. In the next chapter, the analysis is extended to consider the development of worker identities and workplace cultures.

# Chapter 5

# How individuals influence workplace practices, and how work can change worker dispositions and identities

## Introduction

In the previous chapter, we showed how the ways in which workers learn and work are strongly influenced by their prior lives outside the workplace. Now we wish to look at the relationship between individual workers and learners and their workplace activities and experiences in a different way. For through their participation in working practices (including learning), individual workers contribute to the ongoing reconstruction of those workplace practices and, also, in the progressive development of their own sense of identity. First, we draw upon the evidence from the projects in the Research Network to examine the ways in which a worker becomes part of and influences the workplace.

## Individual workers and the production and reproduction of working practices

### Newcomers can change workplace practices

When a person starts in a new job, they enter a world that is at least partly different and even strange. To succeed, they have to learn to fit in—to belong or, as Lave and Wenger (1991) suggest, to become full members of that workplace community. There is a significant volume of research and writing that considers this process for young people entering work for the first time, for example through official or unofficial apprenticeships. In our research network, this sort of beginner induction was a prime focus of the research by Fuller and Unwin on modern apprenticeships in the steel industry. Two of the other studies also focused on newcomers, but not of the conventional apprenticeship kind. Evans and Kersh examined the ways in which mature learners on a college course returned to employment after a significant career break.

*Lead authors: Phil Hodkinson and Heather Hodkinson*

In effect, they were entering a new workplace as a newcomer, despite being mature adults with significant if diverse experiences behind them. Senker examined a program called the Teaching Company Scheme. In this scheme, a recent graduate is placed in a host company on a temporary basis—usually a year. The graduate is new to the company and, therefore, like all other newcomers, has to learn how to belong, for the period of his or her involvement. One of the purposes of the scheme is to give such graduates real experience of working at an appropriate postgraduate level, following their university studies. However, the scheme has an interesting second purpose, for the graduate is supposed to carry out a project for the company, and in so doing, contribute to solving a company problem with the intention of changing some aspects of existing working practices. An example of the work of this scheme is given in Box 5.1.

---

**BOX 5.1**

### *An example from the Teaching Company Scheme (TCS): The case of Andrew*

The Semico TCS scheme was designed to reduce lead times, to improve quality, and to reduce manufacturing cost. Andrew, the TCS Associate, needed to know how the company operated, how parts were manufactured. There was a lack of information on how long each job takes. The workers filled in time sheets for costing out, but this was not in the right form for production management. The production-management information was all in people's heads. Different people were classifying things differently. Andrew did a mini-project on how long it takes to manufacture a part. He had to learn what was happening in the clean room, how long each piece takes in manufacture, how clients set up bills of materials. He mainly learned all this from colleagues here. The Works Manager thought that Andrew's learning could have been improved with more "front-end experience." With hindsight, he would have suggested that Andrew should spend more time on the shop floor, or in the planning office. Andrew had taken too much of a top-down approach, and he should have been in a position to look at the situation from a bottom-up perspective as well. Andrew should have spent two months in the planning office or on the shop floor.

Through participation in the TCS, both the company and the graduate are supposed to learn from each other, and the scheme deliberately uses newcomers to attempt to change existing working practices. However, the results of this change-agent role depend on complex interrelationships between the individual graduate, the project being developed, other workers and, perhaps especially, managers in the workplace, and the existing working culture and practices in which the worker is located. Put differently, the graduate needs to become embedded into the existing workplace culture and community if the project is to have any chance of being effective in introducing change. Issues such as the graduate's prior and possibly tacit knowledge and skills, and his or her dispositions toward the workplace, the project and his or her own learning are significant, in ways described in the previous chapter. That is, the individual graduate can make a difference to the success or failure of the scheme, but so do many other factors that lie outside her or his control and even influence. This is further confirmation of what is perhaps the main theme of this book—that workplace learning is relational and no single factor can be identified as being the most important.

Even when there is no intention that newcomers should change the culture and practices of the workplace, it often happens. For example, many of the apprentices in Fuller and Unwin's study were engaged in teaching as well as learning (Fuller and Unwin 2004). That is, as well as learning from their more experienced colleagues, as the traditional apprenticeship model suggests, they often helped out each other and other senior workers with specific problems or tasks. An obvious example, which also occurred in Hodkinson and Hodkinson's study of school teachers, was the way in which younger apprentices or student teachers had more confidence and experience in using computers and IT more generally than did their older worker colleagues. Unlike the TCS, there was no official agenda involved here, nor any intention on the part of either the older workers or the apprentices to change working practices. Rather, this was an informal, often unrecognized, contribution to the learning of those more experienced older workers, which changed how they did their work, though often in very small ways.

### Learning is not just for beginners

One of the common mistakes about learning, and perhaps especially about learning at work, is the assumption that it is something which is only done by beginners. Indeed, Boud and Solomon (2003) found in a study of Australian colleges that experienced workers resented being labeled "learners," because that somehow implied that they were not competent in their jobs. There are some studies of the ways in which experienced workers continue to learn, and that was the central focus of three of the studies in the Network. Senker examined the learning of domiciliary careworkers, people who supported people caring for others in their own homes. Rainbird and Munro examined the learning of cleaners and careworkers in institutional settings. Hodkinson and Hodkinson studied the learning of experienced secondary school teachers. We have discussed elsewhere the unequal access to learning at work, and some of the reasons for that inequality. Nevertheless, these studies reveal that most if not all workers learn at least to some extent. One way of considering their learning is in relation to the ways in which individual workers contribute to both the preservation of existing working practices and to changing them. Both preservation and change are integrally linked to workplace learning.

In the study of school teachers' learning, these phenomena could be seen in the cultures of the different subject departments. We have already made brief reference in the previous chapter to the ways in which the three art teachers' dispositions and actions were mutually reinforcing in the establishment and maintenance of a culture of collaborative exploration and innovation. This was helped by the stable nature of the Department. These same three teachers had worked together for fifteen years. They had forgotten how this mode of working/learning had come to be established. What was clear was the strong synergy between individual teacher dispositions and the collaborative culture that they had constructed. So deeply entrenched was this culture that there was no strong, explicit leadership. The Head of Department's role was to keep the organization running smoothly with the cooperation of the other two. At a time when the Head of Art was off sick for a term, there was no significant change to departmental culture or working practices. Aspects of school organization, the cultural practices of art as a discipline, and even the physical layout of rooms where they worked all contributed to the working and learning environment in the department. But above all, it was the coproductive practices of the three teachers, drawing from and reinforcing their individual but very similar dispositions that were key to understanding why the working practices and learning in this department was distinctive from that in the others that were studied (Hodkinson and Hodkinson 2003).

In contrast, the Music Department, forcefully led by Steve, had a much more structured and planned approach to continual teacher learning. This culture was also highly collaborative, but Steve deliberately constructed and enhanced such ways of learning, for example by regularly taking student teachers in pairs so that they could learn from each other, but also so that the whole department would learn from their presence. The other music teachers contributed to this learning culture by participating enthusiastically in a wide range of activities. Students and new teachers who joined the department rarely had a problem learning to fit in with this set-up. One experienced teacher who moved to the department came specifically because he wanted to enhance his own teaching by joining this well-respected set-up. Newcomers have brought their own individual strengths to the Department and shared them as part of this collaborative culture. However, one part-time teacher who did not really fit in with these ways of working, did not stay very long. Steve's strong leadership brought the explicit focus on teacher learning, showing the significance of his individual dispositions, combined with his status and power as Head of Department, that established such a positive learning environment in the Music Department. But this could only be achieved with the collaboration of others, and the successful freezing out of the occasional teacher who did not fit.

The IT Department was different. The Head of Department, James, was young and dynamic, wanting to impose his views and approaches on all aspects of their work. He himself learned a lot from the former Head of Department, now a senior teacher, and passed on some of his own ideas, especially through mentoring sessions, to new members of the Department. Nevertheless he described his own learning mainly in very individualistic ways—enjoying responding to challenges, enthusiastic about new books, courses and internet information on his subject. The Department's teaching took place in widely spaced areas of the school and the staff met either by design when there was something specific to sort out or in passing in the main staff common room. Other teachers in the Department had settled to being broadly comfortable with this individualistic approach, one by developing stronger allegiance to the staff in her second teaching subject. Thus, the synergies within the Department were very different to the close collaboration of music and art. History, as we have already seen, was different again, the teachers being happy to cooperate at times but never generating any close collaboration, partly because of the ways their differing dispositions balanced each other.

It is within small working groups and teams, like these secondary subject departments, that the impact of individuals on working practices and upon workplace learning can most easily be seen (Hodkinson and Hodkinson 2004). However, it is important not to lose sight of organizational and structural factors. In the case of English secondary schools, this can be seen in two ways. First, as Box 5.2 makes clear, all these different departments are part of a very similar organizational and occupational culture and practice. If we only considered these more macro-features of the teaching occupation, we would expect strong similarities between all school teacher practices and learning. As the account in Box 5.2 makes clear, there are indeed strong common patterns across all the departments that Hodkinson and Hodkinson studied. However, if we do not incorporate the dispositions and actions of individual teachers into our understanding, the differences just described cannot be fully explained.

These more macro-features of secondary teaching as a working practice are relevant in a different way. Within English secondary

---

**BOX 5.2**

### Common working practices in English secondary school teaching

Teachers' work in English secondary schools strongly patterns workplace learning opportunities. The day is divided up into lessons. The number of lessons and their exact length varies from school to school, but five lessons each of one hour is common. In addition, pupils will meet with a tutor for one or two short form periods, where registration takes place and notices are given out. There is often an assembly at the start of each day, and a lunchtime plus one or two additional breaks, when pupils get free time. This means that a teacher's time is closely regulated, from a short staff meeting before assembly, right through the day. Teachers work alone in lessons, except where auxiliary help is provided—for example for pupils designated to have special educational needs. It is very difficult to get time off from school routines, as to do so requires the work to be covered by another teacher. Times when teachers can interact with each other are breaks and lunchtimes, and occasionally after school. However, these times are also used for official duties and sometimes for formal meetings. In essence, therefore, there is more teacher interaction with pupils than with colleagues.

In recent years, the level of control of schools in England by central government has increased, and new initiatives are frequent (Helsby 1999). Much of the secondary school curriculum is dictated by government policy. There have been directives to increase the teaching of literacy, numeracy, citizenship, and computer use across other areas of the curriculum. Recently, the syllabus for external examination of older pupils has undergone considerable revision. All these policies require teachers to learn to do things differently. There have also been recent initiatives directly related to teacher learning. A three-year funded scheme for teachers to learn to use computers in their jobs coincided with our fieldwork. A performance-management scheme has been introduced with the stated aim of encouraging teacher development, related to extra salary payments. Individual schools must have development plans based around government policy, and individual targets in the performance-management scheme were generally expected to match the school's priorities. A number of days were set aside every year for teachers' development work, with no pupils present. This often involved school-wide sessions on topics which were new or where a skill deficit was perceived. Amongst others, we observed sessions on the introduction of performance management, on teaching literacy and numeracy across the curriculum, and on the introduction of a key-skills curriculum for seventeen-year-olds. There were also chances for departments to work on issues of more immediate relevance to themselves. Planned learning opportunities for all the teachers included the computer-learning sessions, and occasional off-premises courses with teachers from other schools. Most frequently, these concerned the teaching and marking of work for external examinations.

Such pressures and organizational features resulted in common approaches to workplace learning from most teachers in our study. They all taught separate classes behind closed doors and learned about teaching by teaching, in ways that they often described as "trial and error." These are consistent with Beckett and Hager's (2002) account of hot and cold judgment-making, involving "feedforward," or anticipation of future activities, as well as reflection on previous experiences—feedback. The teachers were mainly enthusiastic about their academic subjects, wanting to learn more about them and about teaching them, hoping to inspire their pupils.

> The teachers described learning from books, journals, television, the internet, courses, and exhibitions. They had to respond to externally imposed initiatives, sometimes having to do something new where there was no established expert, but colleagues within and beyond the department to work with. Such initiatives might not match individual or departmental agendas for development but were carried out because otherwise pupils, whose learning is the end product of the work, would lose out.

schools, the subject department has been long established as one of the prime units of organization, and hence a prime location for teachers' work and learning. This is linked to the entrenchment of a school curriculum based upon separate subjects; the deep identification of most secondary school teachers with the separate subject disciplines in which they studied at university, and the development, since World War II, of a middle-management structure in secondary schools, which was primarily, though not exclusively, focused upon subject departmental responsibilities. It is in the departments, for example, that first-order decisions are made about the allocation of classes to teachers, and about the nature and distribution of teaching resources, including who gets which teaching room(s) to work in, as well as the stocking of materials, books, etc. Furthermore, teachers are middle-class professionals, and departmental teams share the same subject identities. This may explain why many secondary school Heads of Department are seen primarily as colleagues by other departmental members, despite the hierarchical power differentials between them. In many other workplaces, this sort of collaboration between a middle manager and workers is much more difficult to achieve. It is this dominance of the subject department that permits and encourages the sorts of cultural differences found by Hodkinson and Hodkinson, and that structures the types of impact that individual teachers can have on their own working practices and learning. Secondary schools in other countries and primary schools in England do not share that form of structural organization.

The fact that secondary school subject departments are specific and localized in their nature, means that the types of co-construction of working practices found by Hodkinson and Hodkinson are partly unique. However, this does not mean that it is only in such situations that individual workers contribute to the preservation and change of working practices. Rather, it means that the particular ways in which such co-construction of working cultures takes place will vary from occupation to occupation, and from workplace to workplace. Individual workers also contribute to wider organizational and occupational practices, not just those of small working teams. This can be illustrated from two of the other studies in the network. Fuller and Unwin found very different types of working practice in relation to apprenticeship in the four steel companies they studied, as was described in Chapter 2. In one firm, the apprenticeship was particularly successful, partly because of the way in which workers and managers alike valued and understood the importance of the apprenticeship as a learning experience. Many of them had been through a similar process in the past, and many of them had worked in the same firm for a considerable period of time. That is, despite all the changes to the context of the firm and to its working processes, the individual workers and managers contributed to the preservation of well-established and deeply rooted attitudes and practices toward the training of apprentices. In Senker's study of the Teaching Company Scheme, which was described earlier in this chapter, the ways in which managers and sometimes other workers understood the purposes of the scheme, the ways in which their established practices either dovetailed with the scheme or made its accommodation difficult, were important factors in determining its eventual success.

Put differently, the extent to which workers support and reinforce or seek to undermine and change existing modes of working, is probably more important that the actions of any one newcomer in determining the nature of working cultures. This can also be seen in the case of the secondary school history department, which is described in Box 5.3. Here, it was the complex interactions between several individual

---

**BOX 5.3**

### *The History Department*

The Head of Department, Sam, was fairly new at the start of the research. He valued people's right to work in their own ways, believing they probably achieved more as a result. He had worked in a more collaborative climate elsewhere than he found in the History

Department when he joined. He wanted to achieve closer collaborative working here, but in spite of making some structural changes, did not significantly affect the Department's working culture. At the start of the research, history was taught by three full-timers, a part-timer, and a number of teachers from other departments taking one or two lessons each. Three teaching rooms were focused on one corridor with a small office, with a fourth room elsewhere. Sam used his influence to consolidate the history teaching area, and to replace the part-timers with a new full-time historian. But two and a half years on, the Department had not moved toward closer collaboration. The teachers got on well, they valued one another's contributions, they worked together well on specific tasks, for example to plan a new course. But formal meetings were unpopular with several of them, and informal meetings were infrequent, in spite of the proximity of the teaching rooms. The teachers dispersed to different staff rooms, the library, and the smoking room.

Jasmin started at the school at the same time as Sam and, like him, would have preferred more collaboration, but a temporary pastoral role took up much of her nonteaching time. In the second year, she moved to part-time working and became a more marginal member of the Department (see Box 5.5). She felt this, and would have valued more meetings to discuss both policy and practicalities. She now consulted most with another experienced teacher, Malcolm, rather than Sam. They were both smokers and met informally in the set-aside smoking room.

Malcolm was a senior member of the Department, but without official responsibility. He had been in the school longer than Sam and taught the relatively prestigious sixth-form courses. He had suffered a series of career setbacks, including not being awarded the Head of Department job when it became available. He had a cynical attitude to most new initiatives, complying only where he saw it as directly necessary—for example, to achieve successful teaching and better exam results. His attitude to learning was that it was achieved by getting on with the job, with a class, in his own classroom. Recognizing Malcolm's strengths as a teacher, Sam had not directly challenged his ways of working, but influenced them indirectly through the introduction of attractive new teaching materials. He now benefits from Malcolm's cooperation when there is something they both recognize as important to plan.

The new full-time historian was shy, and she disliked the staff-room where the others would meet occasionally. She spent some time in mentoring sessions with Sam and appreciated his help. However, she only mixed with the other historians occasionally, and, instead of helping to pull the staff together as Sam had hoped, she reinforced the more isolationist aspects of the culture. She often spent lunchtimes shut in her own classroom. She came into this loosely integrated culture and worked and learned in that same way.

Put differently, it was the interrelationship between these individual teachers, with different preferences, different experiences, and different ways of working, that produced the particular working practices of the History Department. These practices, in turn, influenced the opportunities to learn for those staff. They had less opportunities to learn from each other than did teachers in art or music. (See Hodkinson and Hodkinson 2004b for further details about departmental cultures and their effects on learning.)

teachers that co-constructed and reconstructed the culture and undermined the efforts of a new head of department to make significant changes.

### Workers' personal and career interests

In co-constructing working practices, individual workers have differing personal and career interests. Within any group of workers, not everyone wants the same things. Perhaps more importantly for some management literature, workers often legitimately want things from work that differ from their employers' assumptions. This can be seen in other studies than ours, such as the work of Margaret Somerville, in relation to New South Wales coalminers, where, for example, the deliberate engagement with dangerous practices that breached employers' health and safety procedures were a key part of their masculinist and macho sense of identity and belonging (Billett and Somerville 2004).

With the network projects, the findings of Evans and Kersh in tacit skills and work reentry show that employees evaluate their workplace environment by criteria such as opportunities for career development and personal development. They experience their working environment as restrictive if there are no, or only very limited, opportunities for their professional development. In such cases interviewees stressed that they felt that their work was stagnant, and they were just performing their duties without any long-term benefits either for their companies or themselves. However, the interviews also confirm that employees can sometimes facilitate their workplace being or becoming an expansive environment by taking initiatives, enquiring about opportunities for their professional development and further training, learning from their colleagues, etc. Diana, whose experience is discussed more fully later, was very enthusiastic about undertaking further learning. When she had her job interview, she inquired about opportunities for workplace learning. When she got the job, she took the initiative and reminded her employer about what was said at the job interview: "she [her manager] said 'Oh, well, you've given me some food for thought,' and as a result of that I have been allowed to do the [. . .] Diploma in Management Studies."

Mary also took the initiative in order to get opportunities for workplace learning. As a result of her negotiations with her managers, she succeeded in getting financial support from her employer that enabled her to undertake a course, Certificate for Women in Management:

> at the moment I think I have got to be proactive and say what I want, which is what I've done about this course. I saw the course advertised, I saw its capacity and I applied for it and asked for support from my employers and they gave it; they've paid for it.

A few proactive employees in an environment that promises a degree of expansiveness can further promote that culture. Other employees who experience their workplace environment as restrictive do nothing to try to change it. This could reflect feelings of powerlessness; it could reflect a lack of the requisite personal attributes; it could reflect existing attitudes in the workplace and amongst colleagues. Irene felt indifferent about her job and not really interested in using or further developing her skills, thus contributing to the restrictive nature of that environment.

### The significance of external pressures

Of course, it is not only the actions and dispositions of individual workers, even taken collectively, that sustain or change working practices and cultures. As has been explained in relation to English secondary school departments, and explored more fully in Chapters 2 and 3, the sorts of working practice described in this chapter are also dependent on powerful forces that are external to the actions of the workers themselves. One of the sites studied by Fuller and Unwin provides an example of an environment where the continuity of workplace culture had been challenged by its sale, a few years ago, to another firm. Several employees already had long service with the original family-owned-and managed company. The family sold the business to a company based some 50 miles away, and, since then, the site has been managed as a "satellite" operation which functions to produce and supply parts to the "parent company." Many of the employees of the original company still felt an affiliation to the product name which they helped to create and which now has become subsumed within the identity of the larger enterprise of which they have become part. These employees preferred the autonomy that they felt they had when they were part of the family firm compared with the status of supplier that they had at the time of our study. Although the parent company has a strong track record for training and development and for providing employees with opportunities for progression, it has struggled to create the infrastructure and culture necessary to support an expansive approach in the firm it has taken over, partly because of the dispositions of the workers in that firm. This adds to some employees' suspicions that the parent company is good at the rhetoric of employee development but less successful at its practical implementation.

What this example demonstrates clearly is that neither the new employer nor the workers, wedded to the values and practices of the original firm, were in full control of the situation. Rather, there was an unequal power struggle. The new employer had the power to impose new forms of organization and management and to change many aspects of daily working routines. They did not have the power to convince their acquired workers that these changes were appropriate. The values and practices carried over by those workers from the original firm formed a cultural resistance to the new employer. This took many and varied forms, including what is sometimes termed strategic compliance—going along with the letter of an instruction, without subscribing to the embedded values and purposes that supposedly underpin it.

## Workplaces and worker dispositions and identity

Learning at work entails much more than changes to working practices, although for many employers and for much of the HRM literature, using learning to improve performance is the dominant interest. In addition, people learn through their working experiences in ways that can sometimes be of significance for their wider sense of identity and life experience. (See Box 5.4, for an explanation of identity.) In effect, this is the reverse of the situation as described in the first part of this chapter. Now, we need to focus on the individual as learner, not as contributor.

In making this reversal, it is important not to exaggerate the separation between the individual worker and their place of work. Whilst at work, people are integral parts of the workplace community. The nature of their position and involvement varies considerably from person to person, and some temporary or short-term contract workers may never be more than peripheral. However, whilst there, they become part of that workplace. To take the opposite extreme, there are people who are deeply enmeshed in their place of work. They may have been there for a considerable time, or may be in a position through which they have invested a lot of capital and effort in the nature of the workplace, its culture, and community. However, even for people of this latter type, they still have a life outside work, a life that predated their belonging to the current workplace, and will often have a life after the current workplace—either through a future job change or retirement. Put differently, people are both part of their place of work and separate from it.

---

**BOX 5.4**

### *Dispositions and identity*

There is a large and diverse literature on identity, with which we do not engage here. However, what is clear from our data is that workers have a sense of who they are whilst at work. Furthermore, this sense of who they are is partly learned through the process of participation within the workplace. This sense of worker identity is partly self-constructed (Giddens 1991) and partly ascribed by others. Central to it are both a sense of similarity and association with fellow workers with whom a person feels some common feeling, and also a sense of difference from groups of others. As Giddens suggests, any sense of self is as much subconscious or practically conscious as it is discursive or explicit. Obviously, a sense of worker identity is not only constructed in the current workplace. Rather, people bring an existing sense of self, which can change and develop once at work. Equally obviously, a person's identity at work may differ significantly from other identities—for example, at home in the family, or at leisure.

Another way of looking at the sense of self is through what Pierre Bourdieu (Bourdieu and Wacquant 1992) terms "dispositions." These are also largely tacit, but orientate our thoughts and actions in any situation. Like identity, dispositions are grounded in the whole, embodied person. Like identity, they are a partial reflection of the social structures we inhabit, and those structures operate through and within us partly by means of these dispositions. In most conceptions, both identity and dispositions are deeply established and difficult to change. However, they are not fixed, and our lives are not determined by them. In this project, we found evidence of some of the ways in which learning and practicing at work resulted in partial reconstructions of people's dispositions and working identities. That is, through learning at work, they were becoming someone slightly or even significantly different from before.

This means that the relationship between work, learning at work, and a person's identity is complex. Our research data shows that this relationship can also change over time, as either work or the person (or both) change and evolve. The example already described, of a steelworks that changed ownership, illustrates one example. In this case, the changes to the firm had significant consequences for the identities of the workers, who found that the relationships they had had with the previous employer were now overturned.

The five research projects that make up the Network all focused on workplace learning. Consequently, our data is much sketchier on the ways in which workplace identity interrelates to processes of identity formation outside work—for example, in the family, through issues of personal health, or through leisure activity. However, in one or two cases, the relationships between family and work were identifiable. One such case, which also shows a changing relationship with work and consequently identity at work, is that of Jasmin, shown in Box 5.5.

Jasmin's story is an extreme example of the impact of workplace learning on workplace identity. During the time of our fieldwork, she learned to become more aware of ethnicity issues in the school and in her own participation in it. She also learned through her experiences that she was a less confident and successful teacher than she had previously supposed. We are not making a judgment here about her actual teaching ability. When we met her again, two years later, these problems were well behind her, and she could see herself as successful once more. However, during that difficult time, she learned a deep lack of self-confidence, which, linked with the illness, at one time threatened her teaching career.

---

**BOX 5.5**

*Jasmin's changing identity at work*

Jasmin was a history teacher of South Asian ethnic origin, in the Hodkinson and Hodkinson study. At the start of the research, she was successful, enthusiastic, and ambitious, and had recently had "excellent" assessments from an official school inspection. She had started at the school two years earlier, at the same time as the Head of Department, Sam. She was his preferred confidante on work matters, appearing central to the Department's operation. She had temporary additional responsibility for pastoral care and was elected by the staff onto the School's governing body.

Toward the end of the fieldwork, three years later, things have changed. Jasmin became ill and was unable to complete the teaching on some important courses. This absence through illness meant that she could not always be relied upon. She was a less confident teacher and had more problems with pupils. As a result, she changed from teaching full-time to part-time. She was less central to the Department, and her learning opportunities were much more restricted.

The longitudinal nature of our fieldwork meant that we had tracked the changes for Jasmin over this time. In a later conversation with her, after the research had formally finished, we were able to construct the following explanation for her changed identity at work. There were four completely interlocked strands to this explanation.

### A-level teaching

As an ambitious and able teacher, Jasmin had asked to be given some teaching on the most prestigious academic course in English secondary schools—A level. This is a difficult academic course for the most able pupils aged between sixteen and eighteen. Sam readily agreed, and asked Jasmin to teach a new topic: Decolonization. Jasmin agreed, but there were problems with the topic. It was not a particular area of expertise for her, so she had to learn new materials and ideas very quickly. This was made more difficult, because the History Department had no existing materials that she could draw on. Furthermore, she was an Asian teacher with an all-white class, some of whom held race-related prejudices. Members of the class challenged her interpretations of postcolonial events.

This was a difficult group for Jasmin and included several pupils who had been a problem for her in the past, and who had then been allowed to transfer out of her class. Her authority with the A-level group was undermined when some parents complained to the school requesting a different teacher and suggested that the topic itself was unimportant. There were also some tensions with Sam, whose interpretations of postcolonialism were not the same as hers.

### Family and work tensions

Jasmin's family was always very important to her, but required extra commitment after the death of her mother and especially when her sister got married. This led to some lateness (returning from a family home in another town) and absence related to overtiredness and bereavement stress. The English secondary school system cannot make allowances for this sort of thing. Individual colleagues were helpful and understanding. But classes still had to be taught. Losing a close family member eventually changed Jasmin's perspective on work.

**The problems of nonwhite pupils**

Within the school, Jasmin's awareness of the problems faced by nonwhite pupils increased, as did her irritation about the management of such situations. Her temporary pastoral role revealed community problems. Staffroom discussion of "the Asian kids" lumped them all together. Concern about the lack of progression of "Asian kids" was raised by her at a governors' meeting, where she perceived the reaction, "She would say that, wouldn't she?" and it was suggested, therefore, that she take responsibility. However, she also noted that the governors were fairly toothless, and nothing happened about it.

**Structural barriers to personal learning and development**

Some problems resulted from the idiosyncrasies of national policy-making and also school-management approaches at that time. For example, there were two different schemes for enhancing teachers' pay, and Jasmin qualified for neither. She was too old for a scheme that offered enhanced pay for passing through specified quality thresholds, and had joined teaching too soon to qualify for a golden handshake designed to attract older entrants to the profession. Also, at that time, there was no possibility of promotion within the History Department. A national performance-management scheme, which was supposed to help develop the learning of teachers, was not working well, neither providing good feedback nor generating opportunities. Furthermore, the working practices of English secondary schools did not encourage the sort of individual learning opportunity that Jasmin wanted (see Box 5.2). As a result of all this, Jasmin felt that she received no acknowledgment of the excellent grades she had gained in the national inspection.

This complex combination of factors, involving her family as well as school, and closely related to her identity as an Englishwoman of South Asian origins led to a downward spiral of stress and illness. The result, as we have seen, was significant change to her identity at work through this period, together with a changed relationship between work and family in her wider life.

Many of the ways in which identities are learned at work are less dramatic, and they can be seen positively as well as negatively. Diana was a single mother with four children, who was part of the study by Evans and Kersh. Her previous work experience was mainly in administration, including working for a mail-order company, a trust company and the Post Office. Her family commitments made it difficult for her to obtain a formal qualification and to develop her career. She decided to return to studying when her youngest child entered full-time schooling. At college, she started by taking short courses and passing them, which generated a sense of confidence. As is discussed earlier, Diana decided to undertake a full-time course. She completed her Certificate in Management Studies and obtained a position as diversity administrator in a trade union, with further training opportunities.

Different workplaces affected her identity in different ways. She reported her experience as a post-office assistant rather negatively. She said only two aspects of skills development, from a fixed-response checklist administered after the interview, applied to that job. These were "work as a member of a team" and "working to deadlines." She said that other criteria such as, for example, development of confidence in her skills or use of creativity did not apply, largely because of the nature of the job and work environment. As a result, her workplace did not encourage any positive changes in her work identity. If anything, her personality and lifestyle were affected negatively:

> It was so tough and during this time my face became really aged. Some people used to ask me if I was on drugs, because I looked so awful and tired because of the night shift work. I did not attempt to look for another job, because the night shift suited my schedule of running the household and looking after my children at that time.

Her employment at the end of the fieldwork (as a diversity administrator) provided a different situation. Diana maintained that her new workplace allowed her to realize her personal skills and abilities and this led to positive change in her sense of herself as a valued worker. She felt encouraged to take an initiative in various projects and this stimulated her toward becoming more creative, independent and autonomous within her workplace. She was gradually getting accustomed to taking a leading role in a number of workplace projects. In her own words, she would like "to do something constructive, something lasting and really create something for the members." Diana stressed that her employers recognize her personal interests by encouraging her to take on her own initiatives. Diana confessed that she still experiences occasional outbreaks of "lack of confidence." However, her newly acquired experience and self-assurance are becoming more prominent, and she has become confident enough to propose and initiate new projects. She maintains that her work environment stimulates her toward more active involvement, and she is able to influence what happens.

Both Jasmin and Diana illustrate struggles for identity in the workplace. Recognition was important for both of them, as was a sense of self-fulfillment. In both cases, we can see that identity formation and change involve the actions and perceptions of others in the workplace, as well as self-perception and actions of the individual. As Wenger (1998) suggests, the work of identity formation takes place for everyone at work, often in more mundane and less apparent ways. The art teachers, in the Hodkinson and Hodkinson study, were comfortable with their very similar identities as creative-art teachers, as visual thinkers and learners, and as professionals who wanted to do their teaching well and continually innovate, but who were not ambitious for promotion or managerial responsibility.

Of course, work is only one of many arenas where identity is formed, including the family, local community, and leisure groups and activities. For many people, it may not even be the most significant one. There are also wider aspects of identity that cut across many arenas, including work, such as gender, sexual orientation, ethnicity, social class, nationality, and age. Our point here is simply to confirm that when we consider workplace learning and the place of individual workers in that relationship, as Wenger (1998) also argued, identity formation should not be overlooked.

## Conclusion

If we combine the analysis in this chapter with that in the previous one, one of the central findings of this research becomes apparent. This is, workplace learning depends upon the relationship between individual workers, workplace cultures, and wider structural and regulatory concerns. Individual workers are significant in four different ways:

1   Workers/learners bring prior knowledge, understanding, and skills with them, which can contribute to their future work and learning.
2   The dispositions of workers, toward work, career, and learning influence the ways in which they construct and take advantage of opportunities for learning at work.
3   The values and dispositions of individual workers contribute to the coproduction and reproduction of the communities of practice and workplace cultures where they work.
4   Working and belonging to a workplace community contributes to the developing identity of the workers themselves (Hodkinson et al. 2004).

This means that approaches to understanding workplace learning that ignore the perspectives of individual workers are flawed and unbalanced. Approaches to improve workplace learning that make the same mistake are unlikely to succeed. However, the opposite is also true. Attempts to understand or improve workplace learning that overfocus on the dispositions and actions of individual workers are also flawed and likely to fail. The trick is to focus on the inter-relationships between individuals and workplace culture, rather than overfocus on one or the other.

Chapter 6

# Workplace learning

## The direct and indirect impact of policy interventions

## Introduction

An understanding of the impact of government policies is essential for a contextualized analysis of workplace learning. Before we can begin to consider the significance of government policy for workplace learning, it is first important to locate this sphere of activities within the broader framework of the political economy of the State. As we have argued in earlier chapters, workplace learning is in principle significantly broader than VET, which is focused on formal institutional settings and instruction. Nevertheless, the system of VET is a natural starting point for any analysis of the role of the State in workplace learning. This is because these institutions affect both the supply of qualifications in the labor market—in other words, the quality of labor entering the labor market—and the extent to which it is enhanced through structured interventions in the workplace. This is not to argue that individual employers do not make investment decisions of their own accord, but rather that there is a broader framework which structures the courses provided by colleges and private training organizations and creates sanctions and incentives promoting particular kinds of behavior within the firm. Once created, social institutions reflect a particular balance of power in society and are relatively durable.

## VET systems and the role of the State

Discussions of the role of VET systems within different nation-states are typically located within the varieties of capitalism literature (see for example, Crouch and Streeck 1997, Hall and Soskice 2001). These draw distinctions between market economies, in which the State adopts a relatively noninterventionist approach to the affairs of employers,

*Lead author: Helen Rainbird*

including their strategies toward vocational training, and more regulated economies, where the State fixes the "rules of exchange" and imposes obligations on employers and other interest groups. There are other distinctions to be drawn between economies in which the State plays a centralized role in policy interventions as opposed to a more decentralized approach. For example, the State adopts a centralized approach to training in a number of countries where it obliges employers to contribute to the costs of training through a levy on the wages bill, for example in France (see Gehin and Jobert 2001) and in Korea (Yoon and Lee 2005) and in the developmental states of south-east Asia, where it plays a major role in the supply of labor (Ashton 2004). In contrast, in coordinated economies, employers cooperate with each other through business-interest organizations and with trade unions as well (for example, in setting wages for a particular sector of the economy). They may take on a significant, but decentralized, role in the joint management of the training system and in matters concerning the forward planning of labor requirements in the company, as is the case in Germany.

Why do states intervene in the VET system? The classic argument for the involvement of the State in vocational training is that skill formation is an arena in which both market and state failure occur (Schmitter and Streeck 1985). Market failure occurs because employers acting on their own initiative have a tendency to train less than they should in their own best interests. This is because, as Streeck (1989) argues, they cannot tie their employees into employment and can never be certain of realizing the full benefits of their investment. This is because other employers, who do not invest in training, can pay higher wages to ready-trained labor. This "free-rider" problem lies at the heart of employer underinvestment in skills and results in a chronic undersupply of skilled labor. This is the reason why, Streeck argues, "voluntary investment in training, as guided by imperatives of market rationality will produce high skills only in exceptional cases" (1989: 94).

Although market failure occurs in training, it is also an arena for state failure. For training to be relevant to industry, decisions need to be informed by people who understand the needs of their sector. Because state bureaucracies are distant from the practice of the workplace in different sectors, they have poor-quality information about training and learning needs. One reason why many countries devolve responsibility for training to organizations involving representatives of employers, trainers, and employees is to allow this expertise to be mobilized. Insofar as they are representatives of different interest groups who are directly involved in the workplace, they provide a degree of legitimacy for the decisions that are made.

It could be argued that employers are best placed to make decisions about the types of training that are needed and the quality of the learning process. Nevertheless, in many countries, trade-union representatives, trainers, and representatives of government may also be involved. Why does this happen? Teachers and trainers clearly bring a different kind of expertise, which may or may not be related directly to the workplace. However, it is also the case that employers and employees have different interests in relation to training. In order to tie employees into the company, employers try to keep training narrow, or to limit it to certain categories of employee. In other words, their perception of learning needs may be restrictive (see Chapter 2). In contrast, trade unions tend to support forms of training and development that increase levels of skills and their recognition in the external labor market. In this case, their perception of learning needs may be more expansive than those of employers, both in relation to the types of learning (a preference for that which is developmental and externally recognized, which provides employees individually and collectively with greater bargaining power) and in relation to access (entitlements for all employees rather than managers and the highly qualified).

Government also has a role in VET decisions insofar as the State has an interest in promoting the competitiveness of the economy as a whole. Nevertheless, it also has a social-policy agenda and may want to promote access to training and development as a means of integrating the unemployed into the labor market and ensuring that employees are able to update their skills. These objectives pull in different directions. Economic competitiveness requires an adequate supply of skills in the economy. In contrast, social inclusion involves political considerations relating to the division of wealth and level of tolerance of inequality. In this case, access to education, training, and development has a role in combating social exclusion.

Therefore, the central question concerning government policy toward VET is not "Why does the Government intervene?" but "Why does it intervene in this way?" As with any policy intervention, there is a distinction to be drawn between what the policy claims to do and what it actually does, and its intended and unintended consequences. This chapter sets out by explaining the broader framework of VET policy in the UK from the 1960s until the 1990s. It then focuses specifically on recent interventions by the Labour Government since 1997. It then goes on to explore the different approaches adopted to the public and the private sector and considers whether the continuing shift toward privatization of the public sector increases or decreases the capacity of employers to train and develop their employees. The chapter concludes by discussing the limitations of VET policy in addressing workplace learning, arguing that in order to do this, it is necessary to examine "employer demand" for skills and the patterns of work organization that structure workers' opportunities for learning.

## VET policy interventions in the UK in the postwar period

Policy interventions in the postwar period have shifted between a voluntarist approach, where decisions were left to employers, and a more interventionist approach, where the State has played a more active role. In the immediate postwar period, the State was gradually drawn into a more interventionist role for two reasons: First, because educational and industrial policymakers believed that a general process of upskilling was taking place and that this required higher levels of skill and general education for all workers; and, second, because of the emergence of skill shortages. Finn (1987) maintains that this context resulted in arguments for an extended and reformed period of secondary schooling on the one hand, and for the State to take a more active role in industrial training on the other.

### From a tripartite to a neoliberal regime: 1964–1997[1]

The first major intervention by government in vocational training outside wartime was the 1964 Industrial Training Act, introduced by the Conservative Government but implemented by the Labour Government that came to power in 1964. The Act resulted in the setting up of Industrial Training Boards (ITBs) with responsibilities for training in different industrial sectors. This represented a devolved form of policymaking, whereby equal numbers of representatives of employers and trade unions had seats on their boards. Tripartism refers to the involvement of three parties in policymaking: The state, employers, and trade unions. Educational interests also had seats on the boards. The

---

1  The following sections draw on the introduction of Rainbird (1990) and Rainbird (2005b).

ITBs had powers to raise a training levy on all companies defined as being within their scope and to distribute grants to encourage training. In this way, the costs of training were distributed between companies which did and did not train; those which were "good trainers" were encouraged to train beyond their immediate needs through the allocation of grants. In this way, the "free-rider" problem was addressed. Moreover, the ITBs provided a forum for the development of training programs and curricula and the modernization of apprenticeship training and, in some sectors, encouraged small firms to work together through group training schemes (see Senker's history of the Engineering Industry Training Board [Senker 1992], for example).

The levy–grant system was modified by the Employment and Training Act 1973, in response to criticisms from the small firms' lobby. This had the effect of weakening the powers of the ITBs by replacing the redistributive levy with a weaker levy-exemption mechanism. Under this system, firms that could demonstrate that they were training for their own needs did not have to pay the levy. This represented a shift from a mechanism that could address the needs of the sector as a whole to one that assumed that the needs of the sector represented the sum of individual firms' investments. The 1973 legislation also provided for the setting up of the Manpower Services Commission (MSC), which had responsibility for public employment and training services. The training-services division of the MSC took over the administrative costs of the ITBs and provided grants for selected training activities. The passing of responsibility for the ITBs to the MSC resulted in employers perceiving that they had lost their independence and were increasingly becoming an arm of state policy (Stringer and Richardson 1982).

This view was reinforced as unemployment rose and levels of industrial training declined in the 1970s. The MSC introduced a number of "special measures," and by the early 1980s was funding approximately one-third of apprenticeships. Increasingly, this shifted toward social programs with a training content, such as the Youth Opportunities Programme (YOP). When the Conservative Government came to power in 1979 on a program of reducing state expenditure, it continued to intervene massively in training for the young unemployed, because of the political sensitivity of the issue.

The Conservative Government's approach to training was contradictory. On the one hand it introduced measures to deregulate the labor market, linking training and industrial-relations reform, and to reduce state intervention. On the other hand, it continued to intervene in youth labor-market programs, initially through the YOP and, from 1983, through the Youth Training Scheme (YTS). State support for the running costs of the ITBs was phased out, and in 1981 the Government ordered the abolition of seventeen out of twenty-four of the ITBs. Organizations based on employers' associations, known as nonstatutory training organizations, which had no obligation to represent employee or educational interests on their governing bodies, replaced the ITBs in these sectors.

This shift to what was supposed to be an "employer-led" training policy was paralleled by the development of the "new vocationalism" in secondary schools and further education. In contrast to the educational and training policies of the 1960s, which sought to expand provision, those of the 1980s were geared toward narrow vocationalism, courses intended to give young people "realistic" job expectations and, through the low level of allowances paid to trainees, to depress youth wages.

Finally, responsibility for managing labor-market programs for the unemployed was removed from the central state (initially the MSC, which underwent a number of changes before it was finally abolished) to employer-dominated organizations at local level called training and enterprise councils (see Keep and Rainbird 2003 for a detailed discussion of these developments). Under the Conservative Government, sectoral and national coordination of training and labor-market programs was abolished and replaced by weak, employer-based bodies at sectoral level and a shift to uncoordinated Training and Enterprise Councils (TECs) at local level.

King (1993) argues that these developments in VET policy represented a shift from a tripartite to a neoliberal regime, whereby decisions on training were left to the market. This is not to argue that no attempts were made by government to influence VET in schools and colleges, but that outside the education system, employer prerogative ruled. Indeed, schools and colleges experienced a growth in inspection regimes, linked to an audit culture, which in turn has had implications for monitoring the performance of teachers and institutions.

As Power (1997) argues, audit is now ubiquitous in approaches to government management in the West. Writing specifically about education, Strahern (2000) argues that we are now living in an audit culture, where issues of value for money and accountability dominate debates and require a focus on measured outcomes of preset targets. Within English VET, this has resulted in a regime of constantly changing policy objectives and priority targets, policed through frequently changing inspection criteria. Initiated under the Conservative Government (1979–97), this approach has continued under Labour. Thus, the VET system has two types of measure. The first is a requirement for the retention of students/trainees until courses or programs are completed, together with the achievement of the targeted qualification. Funding depends on both these measures. For providers, the most important task has become the completion of accurate (or even slightly exaggerated) student returns, to ensure that funding is maximized. This is further intensified by checks introduced into the system to minimize cheating. The second measure is the inspection grade, awarded after an intensive visit by an inspection team. Preparation for such a visit can take several months and much depends upon the quality of paperwork produced. Recent research suggests that these audit approaches are actually damaging the quality of learning in further education, which remains the largest provider of VET in the UK (Hodkinson et al. 2004). This is because the system forces managers to prioritize short-term financial survival and leads to high stress and low morale for many tutors. The result is significant amounts of underground working—tutors routinely taking on considerable duties that lie beyond their formal job descriptions, but which are central to the preservation of VET quality (James and Diment 2003).

No doubt unintentionally, this approach to VET management reproduces in the state sector the short-termism that has long been known to damage the involvement of UK employers in VET development (Finegold and Soskice 1988). Moreover, as Goodson (2004) points out, micromanagement dominates reform in the public sector and damages employee involvement.

> One paradox at the heart of the new 'free market' world order is that, whilst business is less and less regulated, the public sector becomes micro-managed at a level of minute mandate and detail. Free markets and de-regulation for the private sector; micro-management and reregulation for the public sector [. . .] Workers' missions and projects are being replaced by mandates that define standards and behaviour. Hence, any harmonization between organizational missions and personal motives becomes accidental and haphazard at best, and confrontational and contradictory at worst. This can mean that people working in the restructured public services begin to take their hearts and minds from the enterprise and perform as technicians carrying out the mandates and missions of others in minimalist fashion: 'it's just a job—I turn up and I do what I'm told.' This is a long way from the personally felt, caring professionalism that once characterized the top end of public sector provision.

This analysis must be tempered by two further observations. First, Keep (1994) has argued that attempts to improve the supply of qualifications through changes to the education system and initial training tended to founder on the absence of demand for more highly qualified workers from employers. This reflected the fact that companies have positioned themselves in market segments where competition is based on price rather than on customized products and niche markets, requiring forms of work organization based on higher levels of skill. The British economy has been conceptualized as being trapped in a "low-skills equilibrium," whereby institutional mechanisms reinforce, rather than challenge, low levels of demand for skills. This has been linked to companies' market strategies, where the price of products is more important than their quality. Keep and Mayhew (1999) argue that there are two elements to employer demand for skills. First-order decisions relate to the choice of product market and competitive strategy. Once these strategies have been established, they have an impact on second-order decisions, which concern the way in which work is organized and jobs are designed. These in turn affect the types of qualifications employers seek when recruiting new staff, the ways in which they invest in their training and development once they are in post, and also the opportunities for informal learning provided in the work environment through daily routines and interactions with other workers. VET can therefore be seen as third-order decisions, affecting the supply of qualifications, on the one hand, and the way in which skills are enhanced in the workplace, on the other.

The second observation is that, having dismantled the institutional framework of the training system, the Government developed a system of competence-based assessment, designed to provide transparency for qualifications awarded by a range of different bodies. The system of NVQs provides a mechanism for assessing workers' ability to perform a range of tasks at different levels, mapped on to occupational standards. Existing training programs must map on to the NVQ standards if they are to receive state funding. In this way, the attainment of NVQ qualifications has become a further mechanism for measuring the performance of individuals and institutions.

The key point to emerge from this analysis is that in removing the requirement for employers to invest in training, the Government lost a significant lever which had the capacity to require employers to think about how they enhanced and deployed workers' skills in the workplace. The mechanisms which have replaced it, namely those which affect the providers of VET, only affect the supply of qualifications and not employers' demand for them.

## A more centralized approach: The Labour Government from 1997

Like the Conservative Government before it, the Labour Government has emphasized the responsibility of both employers and employees for training. Whereas the Conservative Government took the view that "developing training through life is not primarily a government responsibility" (Employment Department 1988), the Labour Government has recognized that it is one of the three main stakeholders, alongside employers and employees (and their representative trade unions).

The Labour Government has largely continued the voluntarist approach of the Conservatives as far as training in companies is concerned, but with some significant changes in relation to the role of the State. Although Labour is more favorably disposed toward approaches based on social partnership, it relies on encouragement and financial support for innovative projects rather than an approach based on legal requirements and entitlements. Despite the absence of formal institutions, trade-union and employer representatives have been involved in an informal way in the process of policy development at national level, for example in drawing up the joint Confederation of British Industry/Trades Union Congress report on productivity commissioned by the Chancellor of the Exchequer in 2002 (CBI/TUC 2001).

Skill formation has been a significant concern, and the Government has commissioned a series of reports that suggested the need to do something about training and skills (see, for example, the reports of the National Skills Task Force 2000 and the Performance and Innovation Unit 2001a and 2001b). Nevertheless, the approach adopted has focused on the supply of skills in the labor market, rather than on measures aimed at increasing employers' utilization and development of workforce skills. In particular, the Government has encouraged an increase in the proportion of young people staying in school and further education beyond the age of compulsory schooling (age sixteen) and participating in higher education. It has introduced a number of measures to encourage adults and young people from disadvantaged backgrounds to participate in education.

One of the key features of developments under New Labour has been an extraordinary centralization of VET policy, through the establishment of the Learning and Skills Council (LSC) under the Learning and Skills

## BOX 6.1

### Back to the future: From YTS to apprenticeship

Ten years after the introduction of the YTS, the then Conservative Government announced the launch of the Modern Apprenticeship (MA) in the 1993 November budget speech. Following the dramatic rise of youth unemployment at the end of the 1970s, various initiatives had been introduced to provide work placements and training for school leavers, culminating in the two-year YTS in 1986. All of these were set within the UK's voluntarist approach and, therefore, suffered from variable quality. Despite this, the Conservative Government was still concerned that employers who recruited trainees were having to deal with too much bureaucracy, and so in 1990 ,YTS was replaced by Youth Training (YT), which carried a reduced administrative burden. At this point, the world of government-funded youth training represented a continuum—at one end, there were a few high-quality schemes that mirrored traditional apprenticeship, whilst at the other end the majority of young people found themselves placed with employers who showed little commitment to their training or achievement of qualifications. Interestingly, the introduction of the MA was not designed to tackle these problems. Rather, it was a response by the Government to concerns that the UK was not producing enough people with intermediate level skills (Level 3), in comparison to other countries with comparable economies. The original intention of the MA, therefore, was that it would be a selective high-quality scheme leading to Level 3 qualifications and would reflect the features of traditional apprenticeships: All apprentices would have employed status and be paid a wage by the employer and not an allowance by the State (as was the case with YTS and YT). The use of the term "apprenticeship," which was still highly regarded by the general public, was designed to reinforce the difference between the MA and earlier schemes. At the same time, the term "modern" was used to signal that the new program would be available in a much wider range of occupational sectors than traditional apprenticeships and would be open to girls as well as boys.

Two years later, YT was renamed National Traineeships (NT), which meant that there was still an alternative scheme running in parallel with the MA. NT led to a Level 2 qualification and was in the mold of previous schemes, as young people did not, necessarily, have employed status and were paid a training allowance by the State. Subsequently, further rebranding took place. NT became Foundation Modern Apprenticeship (FMA) and MA became Advanced Modern Apprenticeship (AMA). In 2004, the terms FMA and AMA were dropped, and the Government now sponsors Apprenticeship (Level 2) and Advanced Apprenticeship (Level 3). This means that despite much tinkering with terminology, the fundamental problems facing government-supported VET in the UK remain:

- too many poor-quality programs
- poor levels of attainment and completion
- lack of employer commitment
- lack of progression
- gender inequalities.

It should be noted, however, that despite these problems and the constant so-called reforms, reputable employers still continue to offer young people high-quality opportunities for training and career progression. Much of this goes unreported, as the weak provision still attracts the main headlines.

Act 2000. The national LSC was set up in April 2001 and its responsibility is for the funding of post-sixteen learning, apart from that provided in universities. Since 2001, this new system of LSCs has replaced the TECs (see above) and the Further Education Funding Council, which was formerly responsible for funding further-education colleges. Moreover, the members of the LSCs are appointed to this role and are accountable to the Secretary of State for Education. In other words, they are not present in a representative role for their organizations, but as individuals. The composition of the LSC board (and those of the forty-seven local LSCs in England and Wales) is not recognizable as social partnership: Employers have been allocated 40 percent of the seats, but the proportion of seats allocated to trade unionists is not guaranteed.

In contrast to the devolved approach to policymaking under the ITB system, the LSC operates a top-down approach. The LSC sets the national framework and allocates the majority of its budget to local LSCs for them to determine, within this national framework, how resources can best be used to raise participation, attainment, learning, and skills levels in the areas they serve. It works with a range of organizations, including the Small Business Service, National Training Organizations, the Learning and Skills Development Agency, Regional Development Agencies, University for Industry regional offices, other relevant regional offices, the careers service (Connexions), the Employment Service, and educational institutions. Working with these organizations, it assesses national, regional, sector, and local priorities. It is responsible for establishing mechanisms to ensure that large national organizations and employers are able to liaise with the LSC at a single national point and to provide nationwide arrangements for funding agreements, payments, audit, monitoring, and management information. As a consequence of this highly centralized approach in which few responsibilities are delegated to other actors, "the English state now finds itself locked into a cycle of further intervention in order to prop up/secure earlier cycles of intervention" (Keep 2004: 9). This is because targets are determined by the State "acting in isolation and then imposed on a multiplicity of other actors within a system in which sanctions are often lacking and wherein the State has no hold whatsoever over the actions of one key group of actors – employers" (Keep 2004: 12).

Centralization and absence of delegation of responsibility also characterize sectoral-level arrangements. Since 2002, the seventy-three voluntary organizations that replaced the ITBs are being replaced progressively by a smaller number of approximately twenty-five Sector Skills Councils (SSCs). The SSCs receive government support through the Sector Skills Development Agency, which issues them a license, coordinates their work, and monitors their performance. The SSCs are expected to collect labor-market information, to identify skills and productivity gaps, and to update national occupational standards. As far as publicly funded training and vocational education are concerned, the SSCs are expected to work with colleges, training providers, universities, and planning bodies to ensure that they understand the sector's needs. Although employers and other organizations have seats on the SSCs, they have little scope for modifying centrally determined targets and strategies.

Although the new framework creates the possibility of collaborative action at sectoral level, which is a key feature of coordinated approaches to training, it does not specify any legal requirements on employers that would underpin such an approach. The SSCs are expected to broker "voluntary collaborative action between employers" and to develop a "sector skills agreement for its sector" (DfEE et al. 2003: 54), although it is not clear who the parties would be to such an agreement (Rainbird 2005a). These could involve the promotion of "collaborative action on skills, including licences to practise or operate, skills passports, sector training academies, voluntary training levies, collaborative training programs or action through the supply chain" (DfEE et al. 2003: 55).

In other words, although SSCs have a coordinating role, they are primarily concerned with improving information about skills needs and adapting public provision to meet the needs identified. Their role is to encourage voluntary action, a mechanism that provides no incentives or sanctions to support collective action or training investment. In contrast, two sectors retain a statutory levy under the provisions of the 1964 Industrial Training Act. These are the Construction Industry Training Board and the Engineering Construction Industry Training Board.

There are, nevertheless, a number of ways in which statutory requirements do affect training or competence assessment (and thus, indirectly, training). In some areas of work, there are requirements for training, in particular in relation to health and safety and the handling of dangerous substances (the Care of Substances Hazardous to Health [COSHH] regulations). In the personal social-care sector, discussed in more detail in Chapter 7, there are requirements for workers to obtain NVQs, although it is important to emphasize that this involves the certification of competence, rather than participation in a specific training program. In this sector, there are now statutory requirements for induction and foundation training, introduced by the Care Standards Act 2000. Since 2005, all careworkers must be registered individually, and there are targets for competence assessment so that employers can demonstrate that they have a competent workforce. Competence is certified by occupational standards developed in the form of NVQs. In the care sector, this involves the certification of competence at NVQ Level 2 in the care of the elderly and Level 3 in the care of children.[2]

One consequence of the statutory requirements for induction and foundation training in the care sector is that government funding

---

2  NVQs are awarded at five levels, Level 1 being the simplest and Level 5 the most advanced. Level 3 is an intermediate level qualification, equivalent to an apprenticeship. See Grugulis (2003) for an up-to-date critique.

is available for training and competence assessment for some categories of workers. In some localities, regional networks of private-, voluntary-, and public-sector employers are emerging, supported by the Training Organization of the Personal Social Services (TOPSS), forming the basis for the development of a form of multi-employer cooperation. So, from one point of view, it could be argued that a statutory requirement for workers to attain NVQs has resulted in the availability of training and development, usually targeted at specific groups (eighteen- to twenty-five-year-olds and workers on tax credits). On the other hand, it could be argued that this simply reinforces private-sector employers' reliance on the State and local government for training in a sector where public services have been outsourced to the private sector.

To conclude, the British training system under the Labour Government can be characterized by highly centralized state intervention in the supply side of the labor market. Although there has been a development of national and sectoral bodies, they are severely constrained in their decision-making by targets imposed from above. Given this level of centralization, there are considerable problems with the extent to which training policies are owned and perceived as legitimate by other potential stakeholders in the training arena. It could be questioned whether the State is best qualified to make decisions about training in terms of knowledge of workplace and occupational practices. It is also debatable whether this focus on the supply side of the labor market has contributed incentives to employers to invest in training in their own workplaces. More importantly, there is little support for the development of cooperative relationships at different levels to support curriculum development and innovation to the benefit of their sectors. Although there are statutory provisions in a minority of sectors, these are unlikely to be extended more widely on the basis of voluntary agreements. Under this model, the State is the main provider of funding for training, and other parties have little influence or ownership of training policy.

## The changing boundaries of the public sector: Privatization and the capacity to promote workplace learning[3]

In the public sector, the State is effectively the employer, so there is scope for the organization to act as a "good employer," adopting enlightened management practices that improve service delivery as well as contributing to broader social-policy objectives on social inclusion and widening participation. In services provided or commissioned by local government and in the NHS, attempts have been made to reconcile the political need to improve the quality of services with the economic drive to reduce costs. Workforce development has played a central role in these strategies.

Nevertheless, the public sector is not homogeneous, even though local government and the NHS are both subject to processes of modernization. In local government, a tendering process has been introduced which requires quality and cost considerations to be taken into consideration in awarding contracts. This is known as "Best Value." This has replaced compulsory competitive tendering, introduced by the Conservative Government, which required public-sector contracts to be let to the lowest bidder. This should mean that factors that contribute to the quality of service delivery (for example, having a competent and well-qualified workforce) might contribute to the training and development strategies of private-sector contractors delivering public services.

When local government and the NHS are compared, it is clear that there are different processes at work in the two sectors. The role of local government is shifting from a direct provider to a commissioner of services. This means that an increasing proportion of work is being subcontracted, and corporate HRM and training departments have less scope for influencing training through direct managerial control in the "extended organization," as their capacity to act in a coordinating role is reduced (Colling 2000). In contrast, in the NHS there is some evidence of internalization of formerly subcontracted services.

A consequence of shifting to a subcontract from the direct provision of services is that the commissioning organization loses direct control over the labor process. The contract manager therefore needs to seek mechanisms for assuring the quality of the service provided.

---

3  For a more detailed discussion see Rainbird et al. (2005) and Chapter 7.

Mechanisms for "managing at a distance" might include the requirement for the contractor to have quality-assurance mechanisms for its
management systems. These include the British quality standard
BS5150, the Investors in People award, which recognizes organizational
training systems, or having a workforce which has achieved a specified
standard of NVQ competence. There is some evidence that where training and competence requirements are specified in contracts, this restricts
the levels of discretion they can exercise in their work (Grugulis et al.
2003). The emphasis is on training records and evidence of training
provision to ensure standardization of working practices and to avoid
liabilities. In other words, such developments restrict the opportunities
for informal learning in work routines and also restrict learning to that
which is strictly needed for the job.

Under a subcontract, line managers and trainers can be based at
distant locations, and progression routes into neighboring occupations
are restricted because organizational boundaries create barriers to
mobility.

In the NHS, political considerations are significant (see the discussion
in Chapter 7). The development of an inhouse organization of agency
staff, NHS Professionals, is one example of an attempt to increase
control of standards as well as to reduce the cost of hiring private agency
staff. This has been a site for developing the "skills escalator" approach
to staff development. In this way, agency staff are provided with
mandatory training, which is often not provided by agencies, and are
also able to access broader training and development opportunities
that can provide routes into professional training to help meet staff
shortages. Direct employment and unified management structures do
not guarantee that all staff gain access to training and development,
but the presence of a training function and collective actors—trade
unions—which can make connections within a larger organization, can
facilitate this.

Earlier in this chapter, it was argued that employer demand for skills
and qualifications is linked to the strategy an organization develops
toward the quality of goods and services it produces. In other words, if
the objective is to provide high-quality public services, we would expect
to see this reflected in the priority attached to investment in workers'
skills. When we compare local government and the NHS, we can see the
different political priorities attached not only to the services but also to
the training and development of the workforce. Although additional
resources are being directed into both areas, higher priority is attached
to the NHS. This is reflected in pressures to bring contracts in-house,

where greater control is possible, and greater emphasis not just on training for staff, even on the lowest salary grades, but on broader development opportunities as well. In contrast, in local government, there has been a shift from the letting of contracts solely on the basis of price competition to one where quality is also a criterion. The problem is that "quality" has been interpreted as standardization and has been introduced after years of undermining baseline budgets for essential services through price-based competition. The conflict between providing a quality service and controlling costs has been resolved in different ways in the two services, and this is reflected in different emphases on the training and development of staff and their capacity to progress educationally and occupationally within the service.

## Conclusion

There are many influences beyond the workplace that may encourage or discourage employers' investment in training and the adoption of forms of work organization that encourage workers to learn. The approach to VET policy adopted by governments in the UK since the abolition of the ITBs in the 1980s has been one that has left key decisions in the workplace to the employer. On the one hand, there are no requirements to spend a proportion of payroll on training. On the other, there are few levers for encouraging employers to adopt product-market strategies requiring forms of work organization that generate demands for higher levels of skills and qualifications.

Within these constraints, two main strategies have been adopted. The first, which has been adopted by the Conservative and the Labour governments alike, has been to encourage increasing numbers of young people to stay on in education and to achieve higher levels of qualification before they enter the labor market. The second, favored by the Labour Government, has been to use the role of the public sector as an employer and as a commissioner of services as a means of encouraging investment in skills and training as part of the wider agenda of public-sector modernization. The Government has argued that this allows the public sector to "lead by example" (DFEE et al. 2003). In general, employees are more likely to receive training and development if they work for a large employer, in the public sector and in unionized workplaces. Public-sector organizations are more likely than the private sector to have a strategic plan covering employee development, to have applied for and achieved the Investors in People award, and to train their employees. However, the public sector is not homogeneous: Whereas there are greater pressures to bring services in-house in the NHS, for reasons of quality control, the pressures to continue to outsource are greater in local government. These developments do not always contribute to the development of expansive learning environments at work, either in terms of access to training or to job design.

Of course, individuals may create opportunities for learning within these constraints. Given the increasing level of formal qualification held by the workforce, it might be possible to speculate that new recruits have greater scope to expand their job roles, to ask for training as part of their development-review process, to be mobile within the organization, or to vote with their feet if they are unable to improve their position internally. Nevertheless, as outlined in Chapter 1, there are optimistic and pessimistic analyses of the future direction of work organization and the scope that workers have individually and collectively to challenge the way in which work is managed. Workers' bargaining power is greatest, and so are the possibilities for external mobility, during periods of buoyant demand for labor. This is not the case in a depressed labor market. Finally, some groups of workers, because of the nature of their formal qualifications and the types of jobs they do, are particularly disem-powered and will always find it difficult to overcome structural constraints to learning and job progression. They are, therefore, crucially dependent on the extent to which a range of different actors—the State, the employer, trade unions, and HR and training managers—can facilitate changes in the workplace as a learning environment.

Chapter 7

# The direct and indirect impact of policy interventions

Case studies from the research

## Introduction

It was clear from the five research projects that the extent and quality of workplace learning in all our research sites was being affected, to a greater or lesser extent, by the influence of government policies. This chapter illustrates the impact of policy interventions through a discussion of case-study examples from three of the research projects. The chapter is divided into three main sections. The first considers direct intervention in the UK social-care sector through the development and application of occupational standards in domiciliary care. As this has resulted in careworkers being required to attain National Vocational Qualifications (NVQs), we examine the ways in which the competence-based model has affected both workers and clients. Drawing on research in the school teaching profession, the second section outlines the impact of direct and indirect policy interventions. Finally, the third section considers the impact of subcontracting on learning opportunities and the nature of the learning environment in cleaning departments in the National Health Service.

## Intervention and regulation in the care sector

In 2003, the Department of Health (DoH) issued a new set of "minimum standards" for the providers of domiciliary care, one set of which related to the employment of careworkers (DoH 2003). Ensuring these standards are maintained is the responsibility of the Commission for Social Care Inspection (CSCI). All new care or support workers delivering personal care who did not already hold a relevant care qualification were now required to demonstrate their competence and register for the relevant NVQ (at Level 2 or 3) within the first six months of employment

*Lead authors: Anne Munro and Peter Senker*

and to have completed the full NVQ award within three years. In terms of the care sector as a whole, the DoH set a target of 50 percent of all personal care to be delivered by workers holding an NVQ (or equivalent qualification) by April 1, 2008. In organizations where the 50 percent target had been reached, the employer was required to continue registering staff for NVQs. In addition, managers in the sector were required to obtain a qualification in management equivalent to NVQ Level 4 within five years.

This intervention by government in the training of careworkers could, on the surface, be said to provide a major opportunity for new learning for a group of people who in the past would have little access to formal qualifications. Given, however, that NVQs represent arguably the most controversial government-led intervention in the UK's VET system since the 1964 Industrial Training Act, the imposition of these competence-based qualifications needs careful examination. The decision to set the minimum qualification standard for careworkers at NVQ Level 2 reflects the current government's commitment to a competence-based model of skill formation introduced in the late 1980s. Before we discuss the findings from our case study of the care sector, it is necessary to briefly examine the reasons why successive British governments have remained committed to NVQs, despite considerable misgivings from a range of commentators about the appropriateness of the competence-based model. It is worth noting, too, that some other countries, notably Australia, Mexico, Poland, and the Netherlands, have also adopted and retained competence-based approaches within their VET systems.

It must be remembered that, until 1964 and the establishment of the first ITBs, British governments had stayed well away from any attempt to regulate or intervene in the design and delivery of VET. This was despite continued complaints about the state of VET provision, relative to that found in other industrialized nations, dating back to the 1850s (see Keep and Mayhew 1988, Unwin 1997). In 1968, the Royal Commission on Trade Unions and Employers' Associations (known as the Donovan Commission), mindful of increasing technological advances and costly industrial action on the part of British trade unions, called for radical changes to the way in which work was organized, including an end to restrictive practices such as demarcations in the workplace and the time-served element of apprenticeships (Royal Commission on Trade Unions and Employers' Associations 1968). It also called for "objective standards to be laid down by which qualifications may be judged" (1968: 92–3). As Raggatt and Williams (1999: 20) point out, this was a highly significant comment in that it marked the first "prominent expression of the desirability of basing training on standards." During the 1960s and early 1970s, the ITBs echoed Donovan by drawing attention to the need for improvements in vocational qualifications, as part of their call for better standards in apprenticeships and workforce development more generally.

Whilst the majority of the ITBs struggled to enact significant change, the MSC, formed in 1973, took up the mantle of "standards," and, in 1981, published its landmark document, *The New Training Initiative*, known as *The NTI* (MSC 1981). This proposed that any program of skill training (whether for young people or adults) must lead to the acquisition of "agreed standards of skill appropriate to the jobs available" (MSC 1981: 4). Raggatt and Williams (1999: 29) argue that policymakers within the MSC at the time were influenced by the "tenets of post-industrial thinking" and "the increasing importance of the service sector," and, hence, that a new model of skill formation was required. The immediate context for the NTI was, however, not so much the need for some blue-skies thinking on qualification reform, but the more pressing need for government to respond to the rapid growth in youth unemployment begun in the late 1970s as a result of Britain's economic downturn in the wake of the world oil crisis. The NTI's biggest proposal, therefore, was the establishment of the YTS for school leavers, eventually launched in 1983 as a one-year scheme and then extended to two years in 1986.

At the heart of YTS was the belief that if young people wanted to find employment, they needed to demonstrate "competence" in both job-specific and "transferable" skills. This formed part of a human-capital, supply-side discourse, which continues today. This means that the responsibility is placed on individuals to invest in their own development to meet the needs of the labor market. Meanwhile, governments are reluctant to intervene to encourage employers to increase their investment in training and raise the demand for skills. Finding a mechanism through which YTS trainees could demonstrate "competence" gave the MSC the reason they needed to push forward with the development of a new form of qualification. Introducing a standards-based and competence-based model of training posed a considerable challenge to the existing VET structures, including vocational qualifications which were largely delivered through colleges of further education. Particularly challenging was the idea that competence-based qualifications could and should be achieved through the successful demonstration of job-specific skills and knowledge in the workplace and that experienced employees could act as assessors. These new qualifications took on, therefore, a very different appearance to existing awards which comprised a syllabus outlining the content to be studied and examination questions.

Central to the design of NVQs was the decision to separate assessment from learning. NVQs comprised lists of the outcomes (expressed as "competence statements") which candidates had to demonstrate they had achieved, as well as the related "performance criteria" against which the assessor would judge the level of competence. The competence statements were based on sets of "standards of competence" defined by some 120 "lead bodies" who represented the different occupational sectors. The new qualifications were to be incorporated within a four-level national qualifications framework, subsequently expanded to include Level 5 (professional-level status) indicating associated levels of competence.

The intention was that NVQs would gradually replace the many thousands of existing vocational qualifications, though this never happened and, today, the number of traditional vocational qualifications awarded each year still outnumber NVQ awards (see Unwin et al. 2004).

The separation of assessment from learning meant, in theory, that people who felt they had already gained skills and knowledge in a range of tasks could present themselves at an NVQ assessment centre in order to have their competence checked against the criteria, and so be awarded a qualification or units toward a qualification. This was seen by some trade unionists and adult educators as a positive step in helping adults (particularly in low-grade, low-paid jobs) who had gained skills and knowledge through their jobs to gain formal recognition for their expertise. At the same time, however, the promotion of workplace assessment, over and above the traditional college-based delivery of qualifications in colleges, was seen by some in the VET community as a reductionist approach to learning. For some commentators, a fundamental problem with NVQs became clear during the early 1990s as they became the instrument by which government could measure the effectiveness of training providers involved in all government-funded youth- and adult-training programs. Hodkinson (1996: 122) has argued that NVQs played a central role in a newly emerging model of VET management that assumed that "the quality of provision can be improved through the measurement of outcomes and payment by results within a market context."

Many of the critiques of NVQs appeared in the mid-1990s (see, *inter alia*, Hyland 1994, Hodkinson and Issitt 1995, and Wolf 1995) when the Government's promotion of the competence model was at its height.

Although NVQs have undergone some changes in the intervening years, including an acknowledgement in some NVQs that a person's level of vocational knowledge cannot be adequately inferred from watching them perform everyday workplace tasks, they still adhere to the premise that the assessment of competence can and should be separated from the learning process involved in the development of skills. In one of the very few recent critiques of the competence model, Hager (2004: 410), reflecting on the Australian experience, has argued that both its critics and supporters "have shared certain questionable assumptions about learning that revolve around viewing it as a product." Hence, the supporters of competence are concerned with judging the value of learning by "what learners can *do*" with it (Hager 2004: 411). In contrast, the critics of competence "place special esteem on propositional learning, and denigrate competence approaches for neglecting this favored kind of learning" (Hager 2004: 411). Hager calls instead for a "workable account of competence, one that is highly consistent with an alternative conception of learning that views it as a process (or, more accurately, as dialectical interplay of process and product)" (2004: 411). This view of learning aligns with the main themes arising from the research reported in this book. As Hager argues, by conceptualizing learning as a holistic and dynamic process, the environment in which the learning is taking place, as well as the individual's dispositions and abilities all become centrally important. In their critique of competence from the perspective of the model used in the Netherlands, Biemans et al. (2004: 532) make an associated point when they remark that there is a paradox in the "over-reliance on standardization of competencies," as "the power of competence-based education lies in its context-embeddedness."

Hager (2004) echoes Hodkinson (1996) in identifying the way in which both the Australian and UK approaches to competence remain deeply flawed because they have conceptualized learning solely as product and so have focused only on performance and outcomes. This has occurred because an economic imperative has driven attempts to reform the VET systems in both countries, as a result of which, the development of the competence model was handed over to "people who lacked understanding and experience of educational issues" (Hager 2004: 413).

The NVQ model of competence could be said to reflect an outdated picture of the workplace as a factory production line, where outcomes are fixed and can easily be measured (see Hodkinson and Issitt 1995: 7). Not only is the model problematic in terms of the nature of contemporary manufacturing environments, it is also inappropriate for those occupations concerned with the complex process of caring for people. Whilst social care has to be governed by standards of professionalism that can be inspected, practitioners are constantly having to adapt their skills and knowledge to new situations, some of which may appear to be in direct conflict with or contradictory to the competence statements laid down in the NVQ Level 2 (see Issitt 1995: 78). Issitt (1995) discusses the clash between the positivist, behaviorist, and mechanistic NVQ model of competence and the need for caring professionals to develop what Schon (1987: 6) refers to as the facility to deal with "indeterminate zones of practice—uncertainty, uniqueness and value conflict," which "escape the canons of technical rationality." In particular, Issitt (1995), echoing Jordan (1991) and Kemshall (1993), highlights the dangerous assumption that the NVQ competence framework is objective and, therefore, can adequately equip professionals to deal with issues of equality and discrimination that they will encounter as part of their everyday practice.

As we will see in the next section, the lack of understanding inherent in the NVQ competence model about how people develop skills and knowledge both in and outside the workplace has profound implications for the viability and sustainability of using NVQs as both a regulatory tool and vehicle for workforce development.

## The impact of NVQs in care homes

Our research in care homes suggests that NVQs have been beneficial insofar as qualifications have now been made available for occupations for which no qualifications at all were previously available. There is evidence to suggest that the self-esteem and pride in their work of many careworkers have, therefore, been boosted by the achievement of nationally recognized qualifications. Our research shows, however, that these benefits are being eroded due to the overelaborate NVQ assessment methodology. Assessment to NVQ standards in the care homes we visited appeared to be principally a requirement for staff to jump through bureaucratic hoops and less a requirement to undergo appropriate training or attain standards of performance. Rather than helping to improve the standard of care, the bureaucracy associated with delivering NVQs takes up valuable time. For example, the Manager of a home for adults with learning difficulties said:

> The NVQ is absolutely ridiculous. Just a lot of paperwork. Staff who have completed it see no benefit whatsoever [. . .] I am qualified

as an NVQ assessor and started to assess staff. But it was just common sense and so time-consuming so I got in an outside organization to do it. If you have good induction training and supervision then everything covered in NVQs is covered. And they keep on changing the goalposts. Staff learn much more from doing courses on subjects like communications, working with people with learning difficulties and behavior modification.

This echoes Rainbird et al.'s (2005: 885–901) finding from their research in social care that "some managers in specialist care units feel that the emphasis on meeting targets for NVQ Level 2 diverts resources from more challenging specialist courses which would have more relevance to a particular service." There have been serious doubts since the early days of NVQs about whether the competence-based assessment process is cost-effective (Wolf 1995: 133–6).

A major concern of the careworkers and managers we interviewed was that using NVQs to regulate care homes is not necessarily effective in maintaining standards or preventing abuse. The costs to society can be significant in terms both of diverting care managers, staff, and trustees from their principal work of providing care, and also in deterring establishment of new community-based care organizations. It could be argued that by handing over the responsibility for ensuring the maintenance of standards in care homes to the CSCI, the Government is hoping to deflect criticism from itself to one of the many external agencies it has created (see Crouch 2000). An interview with the manager of a residential home for adults with learning disabilities indicates that the bureaucratic burden could also deter future recruits from taking up carework, and particularly from aspiring to be managers:

I could spend my whole time just sitting behind my desk doing paperwork and not seeing the clients at all [. . .] When clients knock on the door to see me, I often have to tell them to wait while I finish some paperwork. I started work here five years ago. Since then the paperwork has about doubled [. . .] I have a nursing qualification and I did an Advanced Management in Care NVQ. Then I got a letter saying that was not enough. The bureaucracy is taking away what I came into carework for. My deputy thinks about what it would be like to be a manager and sees me doing all the paperwork. It makes her think "do I really want this?"

There are increasingly indications that the regulation of care provision is not particularly effective, and that its "side-effects" are excessive. In addition to the bureaucratic burden of NVQs, care homes are faced with a further set of regulatory requirements. For example, employees, trustees, and even some visitors to care homes now have to be registered with the Criminal Records Bureau (CRB). Whilst vulnerable people have to be protected, the CRB's efforts are concerned with processing virtually empty forms concerning thousands of people, the vast majority of whom are not known to have committed any crime.

In relation to the bureaucracy surrounding NVQs, a task force set up by the Learning and Skills Council (LSC) (see LSC 2002) to examine bureaucracy in colleges, recommended reducing the frequency and amount of testing associated with NVQs. But this report failed to consider the possibility that some of the defects it reported on could be inherent in the NVQ system (LSC 2002). The final report pointed out that "there was a more general recognition that aspects of the qualifications framework simply were not fit for purpose: NVQs/key skills/technical certificates all becoming too paper based for a client group who largely didn't like/ enjoy/succeed at mainstream education" (LSC 2004: 38). Whilst welcome, it is somewhat astonishing that this recognition of the flaws in creating an assessment-led (as opposed to a learning-led) qualifications system has come so long after such concerns were raised almost twenty years ago.

In a review of its activities, the CSCI found that its inspectors spend too much time "ticking boxes" and not enough time meeting the people using care services. Inspectors use a scoring system based on whether each minimum standard is met rather than whether people using care services are getting what they need. They spend so much time carrying out routine inspection visits that they do not have enough time following up complaints; there are variations throughout the country and too often unacceptable quality is allowed to continue too long. The CSCI admits that it is not doing everything right now, and promises to reform (CSCI 2004: 11).

### Case study of care in the home

In our case study of the Caretree organization, we explored the impact of NVQs through the everyday practice of careworkers. The role of a Caretree carer-support worker (CSW) is typically to go into a family home and take over the responsibility of one member of a family (the carer) for looking after another member of the family (the cared-for person) for a few hours in order to give the carer some hours of respite from heavy caring responsibilities. Cared-for people can be of any age, and many suffer from some form of serious disability and may need practically constant care.

The NVQs for domiciliary careworkers are an amalgamation of standards initially developed for residential care to which standards developed for domiciliary care (of the cared-for person) have been added. The assumption behind the standards is that domiciliary care can be treated as a coherent occupation for which generic statements of competence can be laid down. As we will see later in this section, this betrays a serious lack of understanding of the complex nature of the carer's role and of the extremely varied nature of the contexts in which they work.

An essential role of a Caretree scheme manager is to match the skills, experience, attitudes, and biography of individual CSWs to families. Assessing CSWs through the use of any conceivable set of NVQ standards would be inappropriate. Annie, a Caretree scheme manager explained:

> So many different factors affect the care needs that careful matching of CSW to family is required. One CSW could be excellent in one setting but unsuitable to another [. . .] Since Caretree work involves so much variety, the needs are very different from a typical residential care environment in which the carers have total control of the environment.

It is essential for all CSWs to be trained in certain basic skills (for example, first aid, food hygiene, and moving and handling) and all Caretree CSWs are given such initial training before they start work. However, it is also crucially important that each CSW has a set of attitudes, life experiences, and skills which in some senses "match" the needs of the family in whose home he or she works. Managers do not and cannot treat their CSWs as homogeneous members of an occupation. If, for example, a CSW expresses a strong (even absolute) preference for looking after children, the manager will not force her or him to work with aged people. If the CSW expresses a preference for working in one area rather than another, the manager is also likely to "indulge" that preference, especially as the pay of CSWs is extremely modest in relation to the range of skills they deploy. And if a clash of personalities occurs between family and CSW, the scheme manager will attempt to find a CSW who matches the family's needs better.

Boxes 7.1 to 7.4 illustrate the relevance of biography to CSWs' work and learning in numerous ways (Senker 2003). Amongst the four examples quoted, only the last, Denise, even approximates to the NVQ "ideal" of a "general purpose" CSW. It is, perhaps, not surprising that her attitude is the most positive toward NVQs. We have used a mixture of the careworkers' own words and those of a researcher to create a picture of the women's occupational landscapes.

---

## BOX 7.1

### *Careworker: Rita*

Rita has worked for Caretree for five years. She looks after autistic children. One child is "socially not too bad," others don't speak or understand anything. She and her husband are "link carers." Basically, they trained as foster carers and, for example, look after a special-needs child for forty-eight hours. Autistic children are unpredictable. She doesn't do "bedsores" (in other words, she doesn't look after elderly people). She does a lot in the summer holidays—up to twelve hours per day. She may do a thirty- to forty-hour week in the summer holidays, normally she does twenty to twenty-three hours per week.

---

## BOX 7.2

### *Careworker: Joan*

Joan will only look after old people. She has been with Caretree for twelve years. She works thirty to thirty-five hours per week. You need to know how to handle old people to read situations. She can handle looking after old people. Looking after children would be too much of a responsibility. People who look after children say "I don't know how you can look after the elderly." She is mainly dealing with husbands looking after wives or vice versa. She did have the opportunity of doing an NVQ six years ago, and said, "It's very difficult for someone in our situation to do it. The assessor needs to see you in a specific situation several times."

**BOX 7.3**

### Careworker: Lesley

Lesley works for Caretree for ten to fourteen hours per week. The main requirement is for the carer and the cared-for to feel safe with her. "Empathy, nonjudgmental, sympathetic, practical:" these are the main qualities needed. She is learning all the time. Before she came to work for Caretree, she worked in an old people's home on Saturday nights for about three years. She started with Caretree in 1999. This involved toileting and washing. She has no problem with this. She is doing the caring NVQ Level 2. "It is a joke. It is so basic. It is an insult to your intelligence. It would be an insult to the intelligence of a fifteen-year-old." She has done two units so far. The communications one is about how to make eye contact and about smiling. She is trying to work through it as quickly as possible.

> It is like filling in a tax form. It is verbose. It is a waste of time and energy. It has to be done as a requirement. NVQs are not training. It's like going to the dentist, something you've got to get through. You've got to grit your teeth and do it. Some of it is irrelevant to lone workers. You are not working in a care home environment, the case studies you have to study are not relevant [. . .] You are not nurses, although you do some nursing, such as catheterization. Caretree work ranges from sitting to being a companion to nursing. The standards are written for people without any social graces. They are a waste of time, a waste of energy and a waste of money.

**BOX 7.4**

### Careworker: Denise

Denise is atypical in some respects insofar as she works long hours, is happy to care for people of all ages, and, although concerned that she might be too old to take them, is enthusiastic about NVQs. She has worked for Caretree for nearly eight years. Previously, she was a legal secretary and wanted to go back to work after bringing up her child. She had an elderly mum in her nineties whom she looked after for many years, and her own experience of a child, now in her twenties, who has Asperger's syndrome. Looking after her own child and mum was very useful experience and helped her a lot when she first joined Caretree. She works up to sixty hours per week, averaging about forty. She does more hours than she is paid for—"you can't just leave people when their time is up." She gets a lot of pleasure from her work. Her clients are between six and ninety-six. There are nine regulars, five of them children, four of whom have physical disabilities and one who is autistic. The four adults mainly have Alzheimer's. But she knows nearly all her colleagues' clients too. She takes over when they go on holiday. "You need to know about the conditions from which people suffer. You need to know about Alzheimer's—people with Alzheimer's are somewhat like people with Asperger's. They like routine. If you change anything they get disoriented." With the ninety-six-year-old lady, she has a routine of getting her pension, going to get coffee in the same place each week, then going to Waitrose to get shopping (most of which she does not need). Her daughter runs a school, and Denise looks after her ninety-six-year-old mother for ten hours per week—and has been doing so for about seven years. She learns most from the parents of the children she looks after. She has looked at NVQs and thinks they are "wonderful." But she is concerned about costs as "Caretree is strapped for cash." She said she would be happy to seek to acquire an NVQ, but she also said she was too old to do NVQs, and she is afraid of all that writing and learning. She hopes to go on working until the normal age limit of seventy.

In order to explore the relationship between NVQs and the everyday work of carers, we interviewed Norma, a Caretree scheme manager. She explained that although people who come into carework often come in with a "task focus," that is, they are interested in physical care, Caretree is not primarily about physical-care tasks. The most important thing that Norma tells new staff is that they are there for the carer. Some of the best CSWs provide emotional support by listening. Sometimes their work may be mainly sitting with somebody, playing Scrabble, having a cup of tea. Ideally, Caretree would like to provide more training on Parkinson's disease, strokes, and Alzheimer's disease—in other words, the main afflictions affecting cared-for people. Much of this training is available free from voluntary organizations catering for people with such afflictions, but Caretree has to concentrate on meeting the NVQ requirement. Norma did the modules to become accredited as an NVQ assessor, and said:

> The NVQ system is "completely unfathomable . . . open to abuse. I could just sit here and sign my lot off [. . .] Generally getting an NVQ involves assembling two great portfolios. It's quite intimidating. A lot of people come into carework because they do not feel able to cope with written work. The NVQ will discourage people from caring work. Women returners—especially older ones—will be discouraged.

Norma envisages that she will have to send (senior) CSWs out with CSWs who need to gain NVQs, to get them to write witness statements to provide evidence that the competence statements have been achieved. There are, however, difficulties in creating opportunities for CSWs to meet the criteria laid down in NVQ Level 2 elements. At present, managers spend a lot of time matching people and their needs with CSWs with appropriate skills and personalities. The NVQ is too "task oriented." Thus, every CSW will need to have toileting experience, bathing experience, moving, and handling experience. Norma has put aside a budget of £15,000 for NVQs. She said that if she had that amount of money to put into the extra training which they really need, "we'd be laughing."

When the NVQ system is firmly in place, Caretree managers will lose the services of many CSWs, especially older ones. Finding enough people with suitable attitudes and experience to train to do this highly skilled yet very poorly paid work will become more difficult—perhaps impossible.

## Direct and indirect interventions in teacher learning: A case study of secondary schools

In this section, we show how our research findings highlighted the impact of school-management processes and national policy on teacher learning both directly and indirectly. In two secondary schools we studied in England, the approaches of management were slightly but significantly different. Mayfield had a successful and charismatic headteacher. Teachers there seemed more contented with management than their colleagues in the other school, and new initiatives, such as a nationally imposed performance-management scheme, were introduced in a positive way, which caused little friction. There were the usual struggles over resources, but the two departments we studied there felt valued and supported for much of the time. Teacher development was emphasized.

In the second school, Leaside, management had been criticized in an inspection report just before our fieldwork commenced, although the problems were officially overcome within two years. However, the Head resigned and was temporarily replaced by one of the deputies. Teachers here grumbled more about management than did those at Mayfield. There was also a sense that some management-initiated processes were not fully implemented. The structure for professional development was similar to Mayfield, but perceived as less well organized. The introduction of performance management and some school-organized in-service training generated some antagonism and dissatisfaction, which interfered with its functioning. These differences were differences of degree. Overall, there was a similarity of approach, which reflected the strength and frequency of government interventions and regulations. Consequently, it is to this that we now devote most attention.

During the research period there was strong *direct* pressure from government aimed at teacher learning and development. In particular, there was the introduction of a nationally imposed, locally interpreted performance-management scheme and a compulsory scheme for all teachers to learn to use computers more in their work.

Skill deficits are sometimes real, and teachers often want to deal with such problems. All of the Art Department at Mayfield, for example, were aware of the potential of computers in their subject, but were finding the compulsory IT training problematic. They were reluctant to attend distance-learning sessions in the school's computer suites alongside other teachers, finding the situation intimidating as relative novices. There are many specific applications of IT relating to art, which they would have liked to sort out for themselves in their own surroundings with focused support. The fact that there were only two computers in the Art Department and that neither was networked meant that they were unable to make use of appropriate materials, so they had no incentive to use the school's version of the national provision. They were looking for learning involving extended participation, within their own established departmental practices of learning as creative exploration. What they were given was a standardized online training course, with reference to art teaching but without the facilities to make use of the (few, for them) more interesting parts of the material. One art teacher eventually made significant progress, but through buying a computer and art software to use at home. She then helped her colleagues.

In the History Department at Leaside, the teachers were starting with a higher level of computer literacy and had two serious problems. First, they still had to go through the lowest levels of the online training course from which they gained little. Second, they did not have computers in the department to put into practice anything they did learn. They believed that without practice they would forget most of what they learned. At least one teacher felt that it was so much of a waste of time that he contrived ways around the assessment system, which at least partly involved a computer record of time spent.

By the end of the computer-training initiative, the level of IT literacy was higher in the departments in our research, but rarely directly as a result of the imposed course, and certainly not at a level commensurate with the high level of government expenditure. The greatest success came in the Music Department at Mayfield, where they did not follow the system as prescribed. The Head of Music negotiated permission for his department to spend the first allocated training day at one of their homes. There they made use of the expertise of a younger teacher with her own computer, to work together through the first few units of the required materials, digressing where it seemed appropriate to relate to their own departmental practices. Unlike the artists and historians, they already had computers in the department. Some of them put in a considerable effort thereafter to learn to use departmental software by persevering with it when other methods initially seemed easier. The government initiative provided a trigger and an initial working day. The learning culture of the department, the willingness of one individual to share her skills, and the determination of others to progress through practice, led to success.

### *"Formalized" learning for teachers*

There are two major pressures restricting formalized teacher learning. One is time. Teachers are reluctant to leave their classes for their own learning, and, especially in an era of outcome measurement, league tables and inspections, school management is similarly reluctant. Exceptions are made, for example when the learning is examination related. Our schools, like many others, limit the number of teachers who can be off site at any one time. Teachers' time out for learning competes with time out to run offsite activities for pupils. Therefore, most planned teacher-learning activity is located within the five designated days a year when teachers are in school, but the pupils are not. Undertaking planned learning beyond these days often relies on teachers giving up their own time, in the evenings, at weekends or during the holidays.

The second pressure is limited funding. Any money available had to be targeted at government-imposed priorities, and at the school's annual development plan (also government priority related). Money for learning initiated by teachers for their own professional purposes was rarely available. Several of our sample reported being unable to undertake learning they wanted to do in their own time, because there was no funding to support them. This policy approach toward teacher learning presented problems for experienced, successful teachers. There was little policy recognition of experienced teachers' need for the sort of learning that might expand and extend their existing expertise and enhance and sustain their success, unless it clearly fitted a national or school development priority, or could be seen as *measurably* contributing to improvements in teaching.

Government interventions and school-management approaches did result in some effective learning. Many teachers described ways in which imposed curriculum or assessment change had led to effective learning and improved practice. Short courses and in-service provision could be effective on occasions, sometimes partly through providing an opportunity for teachers to talk to a different set of colleagues with similar problems. Short courses were most successful if the teachers valued the content and the way it was provided, and felt valued in the process. They also needed to be able to integrate and adapt what they had learned in ongoing practice without delay. Where management and policy dictate direct interventions into teacher learning, they need to have flexibility built in and clear direct applicability to practice.

There was also considerable *indirect* pressure for teacher learning as a result of national policy. For example, government-led curriculum initiatives and changes are frequent. Thus, for example, over the period of the research, the introduction of Curriculum 2000, a major government-imposed reform of A levels in England, caused major changes to external exams and curriculum content. In order to implement these changes, teachers had to do a lot of learning. The case study of the Mayfield Art Department (see Box 7.5) illustrates the extra burdens facing the Head of Department and her colleagues in having to meet the requirements of Curriculum 2000.

**BOX 7.5**

**_Curriculum 2000: Meeting the challenge_**

The Head of Art at Mayfield School, described the problems of getting to grips with the requirements for pupils to sit a national examination after one year of study. Under the original A-level system, gradual development was possible as the exams were not until the end of the second year. She and her colleagues spent many hours trying to modify existing projects and to devise new ones to fit the Curriculum 2000 specifications. Although they had access to much written material and to courses provided by the examination boards, much of the learning took place in practical working sessions with colleagues and in the process of teaching the pupils. This senior teacher believes that it is only through the experience of seeing the results of exams that they will come to learn exactly what is expected. She described this from previous experience of curriculum changes:

> I think now we need to be looking at, "OK, we've changed, what are the good aspects of this change?" A bit like National Curriculum of what, eight years ago, you know. It was introduced and everybody was like "Oh dear, it's new." After a couple of years, people were then saying, "Oh, it's new, but we do _this_ really well," so I think that's [what] we need to do now, it's new, but how are we going to make it really good?

**BOX 7.6**

**_Using learning for different ends_**

The same teacher may become an examiner or moderator for the new qualifications, which will both result in extra training and increase her experience of what is acceptable through seeing what other schools are doing. She has done the same at GCSE level. In order to provide the best-informed help for her own pupils, she said "I get the opportunity—because I go and see in several schools, you

> get this idea of what the levels and what the standards are." She differentiated sharply between learning that she wanted to do to develop her own expertise and this type of learning she is having to do to comply with new regulations.

This example highlights the policymakers' lack of understanding about the effect their "reforms" have on the everyday practice of professionals and the way in which having to respond to new policies disrupts the ongoing, organic learning which professionals naturally engage in, in order to create space for a different, more reactive and potentially limited type of learning activity.

In the next section, we examine the ways in which government policies have had indirect impact on the work and learning of cleaners working in the NHS.

## Indirect policy interventions: A case study of cleaning work in the NHS

In the UK, the cleaning-industry workforce has fewer qualifications than the workforce generally, yet receives little training. The Cleaning Industry National Training Organization (CINTO) suggest that in 1999 less than 10 percent of the total workforce received any on-the-job training and only 2.2 percent received off-the-job training (CINTO 2001: 18). A higher proportion of the directly employed public-sector workforce holds some form of cleaning qualification than the contract cleaning sector (Pye Tait 2003: 6). A range of initiatives within the NHS have promoted learning opportunities for all staff. Indeed, it seems likely that the NHS provides cleaners with access to more training and learning opportunities than any other sector. However, the extent of such opportunities is affected by a range of indirect policy interventions, such as the subcontracting of work to the private sector. The case studies presented here provide a comparison between two cleaning departments with the NHS, one directly employed and one subcontracted.

Cleaners in the NHS exist at the bottom of an extremely hierarchical service and have often faced the brunt of government attempts to limit the NHS pay bill. In 1983, the Secretary of State for Social Services issued a circular requiring all health authorities to open hospital cleaning to competitive tendering (Munro 1999). Mailly et al. (1989)

argue that even where contracts were awarded in-house, the process of tendering provided management with a lever to achieve staff cuts, work intensification, and changes to work organization. Between 1980 and 1990, there was a 50 percent cut in the number of cleaners in the NHS in England and a loss of 30,000 cleaning jobs between 1982 and 1986 (Munro 1999).

The NHS is also directly affected by political considerations. One example of this has been increasing media attention on the issue of dirty wards in hospitals, leading both the Prime Minister and heath ministers to champion the drive toward national cleaning standards. Cleaning staff are based in Facilities Directorates, and there has been considerable concern over who manages cleaning—particularly in clinical and ward areas. One initiative has been the drive to give some control over ward cleaning to nursing staff. In 2004, the DoH published its *Matron's Charter: An Action Plan for Cleaner Hospitals*, which sets out ten commitments for working toward cleaner hospitals. The Charter emphasizes the importance of domestic service staff, but identifies matrons as being responsible for "leading and driving a culture of cleanliness in clinical areas" (2004: 12). Another response has been the development of the housekeeper role, based within facilities departments but with a specific remit to liaise with nursing staff. It is assumed that nursing control over cleaning would improve the quality of cleaning, but nursing staff have little awareness of the training and learning issues for cleaning staff.

### East Coast NHS Trust

This Trust employed a total of 2,800 staff over thirty-seven sites, from small surgeries to general hospitals. At the time of the research, a reorganization into a new primary-care trust (PCT) was imminent. There were a total of 281 domestic staff and thirteen domestic supervisors. All of the domestic staff were female and all worked part-time. The Trust had a learning partnership with the trade union UNISON and, at senior levels, a commitment to learning opportunities for all. Reflecting a national pattern, training resources had tended to focus on qualified professional staff, and the requirements for NVQ for health-care staff had led to a significant growth in this area. The Director of Personnel explained:

> We said some time ago that every member of staff should have learning opportunities—the domestics as well as the consultants [. . .] Staff who do Return to Learn have come out of school with

not much or didn't make the most of it and end up getting a routine mundane job. Give them a learning opportunity and unlock motivation inside—it's just un-tapping that [. . .] Return to Learn is a springboard to further training.

The Return to Learn program is described more fully in Chapter 3. An interviewee from one of the learning-provider organizations pointed out that management increasingly have to meet targets, for example on NVQ, but have difficulty in getting staff "on the road to learning" and creating a learning culture. The developmental learning opportunities were seen as the first step to get people to go on to do qualifications. However, the Training Manager indicated some contradictions in the requirements coming from government:

> The Government is sending mixed messages. The NHS plan indicates learning for all, but more money is needed for training for ancillary staff. In the past, ancillary staff have been neglected. But the Government also sets financial targets with patient care the bottom line—the ancillary side is where the cuts can be made—either the amount of time to do the job or their training.

As well as general cleaning of public areas and wards, domestics serve food and all beverages on the ward, and collect and wash crockery. The responsibility to serve food began a couple of years before the research was conducted, and previously meals were served by nursing staff. This change resulted in additional requirements for training in food hygiene. Routine training for cleaners included induction, on-the-job training within a month on products, equipment, basic health and safety, color-coding, hazardous substances, and lifting and handling. Such mandatory training was conducted by supervisors, and staff were supposed to receive refresher training every two years. Record-keeping had been "tightened up," and staff had to sign to say that they have received the training. Some off-the-job training was provided for care of equipment and food hygiene—typically a one-hour session each week over a six-week period. Additional training covered areas such as steam-cleaning in theatres, barrier nursing rooms (infection control), and renal units (blood spillage). Procedures had been written for every activity, which the cleaner was "talked through," then shown. Finally, they were given a hard copy of the procedures. All staff were supposed to have a personal-development interview once a year, although a department manager claimed that a lot of staff saw little benefit from these.

There were also a range of more developmental learning opportunities, which were categorized as lifelong learning, open to lower-grade and non-professionally qualified staff such as domestic-service workers. These include Return to Learn, which has been one of the most successful programs, but also communication skills, "Women, Work and Society," and "Brush Up Your Skills" (a series of taster sessions for a few hours covering, for example, speaking and listening, introduction to computers, and "Maths for the Terrified").

The Trust had had a number of notable success stories of career progression—domestics who completed Return to Learn and became healthcare assistants, some of whom have gone on to do a nursing degree, including one porter. Other people have gone on to do further training and moved to new jobs, while others stay in the same job "but get more out of it, and are full of confidence." It could be argued that this Trust had gone some way to creating an expansive learning environment for the cleaning staff. However, there were still a number of barriers to this process. Some line managers had not been "won over" to the value of wider learning opportunities. There were also enormous problems with finding cover for staff who attended off-the-job courses; there was no allowance in the rota for cover for training, only for annual leave. As one line manager pointed out, in a department with recruitment difficulties, "it's people, not just the money."

The Director of Personnel explained that learning opportunities had to marry the needs of the organization and of the individual, but also argued that "If you help someone develop, even if not job related, it makes them a better person, makes them better at the job." One difficulty for supporters of learning is to demonstrate the benefits to the organization:

> There are hard measures, but no evidence—it's more a belief than scientifically established link. Workplace learning makes a team player with lower sickness and turnover rates. But all sorts of other things impact on it—better teams do deal with things like sickness.

A range of interventions may have an indirect impact on the provision of wider developmental learning and the nature of the learning environment. There was a fear that the public focus on dirty hospitals had led to a renewed focus on task-specific training, although this Trust had maintained its commitment to developmental learning. The Facilities Director described the media attention as demoralizing, arguing that costs had been pushed down with competitive tendering and then they were criticized—"We feel we can't do anything right." One response has been to put cleaning under the control of nurses, based on the assumption of a need for "ownership at ward level." However, there was doubt about the ability of nurses to facilitate training and cover arrangements for cleaners. One supervisor said, "Nurses don't want management but do want control." Another asked, "How would the ward sister arrange things like cover, specifications, monitoring, training?"

At this Trust, there was a commitment to the in-house provision of all services and a belief that private contractors provide a less satisfactory service. One of the hospitals had previously contracted out cleaning services, although it had been brought in-house just prior to the research. A senior manager claimed that their profit came largely out of savings on the training budget and that they had provided no real staff development, but focused on very strict and narrow training provision. When the cleaning went in-house, the staff could not believe how much training was available—"They had been there years and were not used to training—it was a different culture." The Trust took over all staff, including the supervisors, and the Training Manager suggested that it was "difficult to change expectations with the same managers in place."

There were also fears about the impact on wider learning of various organizational changes. There were concerns about formation of PCTs, in which control over training for lower-grade staff could pass to people who do not recognize the value of training people in nonspecific skills. Experience had been that cleaners in some of the smaller sites, such as general practitioners' surgeries, got little training. The Training Manager said, "They may not understand the role of developing people—the whole person—a holistic approach. I would hope they see the value but suspect they will only see value in training just for the job."

What became clear was the importance of "learning champions" such as the Training Manager, who were continually arguing the case for learning opportunities. Other champions were the UNISON representatives, who played a key role in the recruitment of lower-grade staff, who often lack confidence, to the courses in the first place. Union representatives were able to reassure and encourage staff who were nervous about learning.

## Clean-Co

Clean-Co is a non-UK-owned multinational company, which at the time of the research had a health division of approximately 10,000 staff in the UK. Clean-Co held the contract to provide full hotel services at Royal NHS Trust, a general hospital, including catering, cleaning, portering, laundry and linen services, some driving, and administration. Clean-Co followed a national training strategy, which focused mainly on statutory training, although the company used the British Institute of Cleaning Standards (BICS) training program and offered some NVQs. Company policy was that every member of staff should have an appraisal review and it was estimated at the time that about 80 percent of staff took part in such a review annually. The company was in the process of training BICS assessors and planned to develop a BICS Centre of Excellence. The assessors would be able to deliver training around ten key tasks, which involve off-the-job and on-the-job training and a practical assessment. The Regional Training Manager described lifelong learning, which is not task-specific, as having a lower profile, although indicated that all staff had been offered the opportunity to go on a basic skills course during work time. There had not been, however, a great up-take of this opportunity by staff.

At Royal, hospital domestic staff were responsible for a similar range of activities to those at East Coast NHS Trust, including the service of meals at ward level. Again, this had created additional requirements for staff to complete food-hygiene training. As at East Coast, the domestic group at Royal was completely female.

A senior manager felt that the political emphasis had moved away from contracting out services within the public sector, which had put increased pressure on the remaining companies to provide a good quality service. In addition, the public concern about dirty hospitals and the risks of infection had a direct effect on the company's allocation of resources to training in the health sector. All bids for contracts have to refer to staff training, and the Manager described their aim to change the whole culture. This had led private companies to pay more attention to training; however, the focus of that training was task-specific rather than developmental, and the development of an expansive learning environment was extremely limited. The main focus was on monitoring standards of work rather than on developing the workforce.

Every domestic had the chance to go through the BICS course, and all staff were expected to be competent in the BICS key tasks. Every member of staff had a training card, and training is tightly monitored and recorded. Training had been formalized; previously, a new member of staff would just go on a ward with another domestic, this had been changed to a supervisory responsibility. Each unit received a quality-assurance visit and had to achieve a certain level of mark. As well as the annual appraisal, individuals had to take an annual exam. Staff had mixed views about the exam, one describing them as "OK" and another as "silly—it's a question of common sense."

It was suggested that the company would train anyone up to any level, although moving beyond supervisory level would have required a move to another site within the company, which could be a considerable distance. This was not possible for most cleaners who lived very locally and looked to occupations within the NHS, not within the company, for progression. The manager added that the company would be happy to train staff in non-task-specific areas, for example in IT, and would pay them overtime to study after their shift. However, there had been very little take-up by staff, and the onus was very much on staff to take the initiative. No cleaners interviewed for our research had taken part in any development activities. There were no union training representatives at the unit, the manager had received no approach from the trade unions on training and development issues, and he had not heard of the Return to Learn program. No training issues had been raised through staff representative meetings. Progression was clearly within the company, not within the hospital. The Unit Facilities Manager described as problematic the recruitment of domestics to healthcare assistant roles: "If a domestic is on a ward and sees a job advertised, a nurse on the ward may suggest she apply—we have lost a lot of good workers to the trust." With a tight labor market and problems of recruitment, there is no incentive for a contract company to facilitate progression through the nursing route.

An earlier problem had been identified as the failure to respond to spillage or mess created after the daily clean. As a result, the "rapid response team" was established. The team had six members, one man and five women, who had been drawn from the catering and domestic-services groups. The team was able to deal with exceptional or unexpected mess, to back up the general staff teams as needed, and to carry out special infection scrubs. They also dealt with periodic jobs such as curtain changes and window cleaning. As generic workers, they received task-specific training in a wide range of areas and received a higher rate of pay. Box 7.7 illustrates the impact of this initiative on one individual.

---

**BOX 7.7**

***Accessing learning: The case of Rob***

Rob started as a domestic on the wards, but felt awkward and out of place as the only man. He then became a porter, a job which he felt gave him more autonomy and more variety—in cleaning, he was always doing the same thing in the same place. Rob applied for the job in the rapid response team, as he thought it would be a challenge, but the majority of the work turned out to be cleaning. He had received training from the domestic supervisor: Manual handling, food hygiene, clinical-waste management, and experience in other portering roles, including the handling of X-rays and mail. He was keen to pursue a career in nursing, but no one had ever spoken to him about wider development opportunities and this would certainly require a change of employer. He was a UNISON member but had not heard about courses through UNISON and had never heard of Return to Learn.

---

Rob's example illustrates a number of the implications for learning in subcontracted contexts. There were no learning champions amongst management or the trade unions. Training, while considerable and well documented, was very much task-specific, and there was little encouragement for wider developmental learning. Progression was limited to the company rather than the NHS.

---

**Conclusion**

The examples described here demonstrate the importance of context and environment to the provision of training and learning opportunities, and to the assessment of achievement. For both the teachers and the care assistants, national regulatory requirements did not fit with the needs of particular workers in particular situations. There are clear limitations to the "one size fits all" approach to training, assessment, and qualifications. For teachers and cleaners in highly politicized areas of the public sector and in the voluntary sector, competing regulations and a variety of targets often result in more developmental learning opportunities being squeezed out. In contracted-out cleaning and in caring, the need for contract compliance led to a focus on task-related training and comprehensive documentation of training rather than developmental learning opportunities. Despite identified benefits to the case-study organizations of wider learning opportunities, there remained a desire for measurable outcomes for such learning. In the case of the cleaners in the private company, the onus was on staff themselves to initiate learning opportunities. Lower-grade staff, with poor educational attainment and limited experiences of learning, are unlikely to have the required confidence. This highlights the importance of learning champions for such groups. For all occupational areas, the pressures of both time and money were a major issue.

# Part III

# The Conclusions

# Chapter 8

# Improving workplace learning

## An integrated approach

## An integrated, or cultural, approach to improving workplace learning

The findings of our research into workplace learning have been explained in different chapters. Perhaps the most important outcome of the work has been the realization that if we are to understand workplace learning, and especially if we are to improve it, it is important to take a more holistic, integrated approach. One way of understanding this is to think of improvements to workplace learning taking place at three overlapping scales of activity. The first two concern the context of learning and the third the way in which individual workers interact with the opportunities afforded by this context.

At the highest level, wider social structures and social institutions can be fundamental in enabling or preventing effective learning from taking place. For example, the extent to which collective actors, such as employers' associations and trade unions, are delegated responsibility for vocational training and enhancing learning and innovation in intermediate-level institutions (for example, at sectoral or local level) will impact both on the legitimacy of these institutions, the resources available for learning, their perceived usefulness, and the ability of the actors to work together at lower levels. This is not just a case of specifying rights and responsibilities, but also of creating mechanisms for establishing the shared ownership of objectives and for putting these into practice. The evidence from our research suggests that, due to the absence of wider institutional structures supporting workplace learning, there is weak support at this level for the development of expansive learning environments in the workplace in the UK.

At a lower level, the nature of the learning environment in the organization is important. It is at this level that a range of local actors

*Lead authors: Phil Hodkinson and Helen Rainbird*

can have an impact on the learning environment. In the shower-fittings company, Company A, studied by Fuller and Unwin and discussed in Chapter 2, there was a long-established expectation that all employees would learn, both in formal learning environments and in the workplace. They characterized this as an expansive learning environment. Establishing such a culture, where it does not exist, is more problematic.

One reason for this difficulty is that, despite the rhetoric about the learning society and the learning organization, for most employers, workers' learning is not a priority and represents a third-order decision. As discussed in Chapter 1, first-order decisions concern markets and competitive strategy. These in turn affect second-order strategies concerning work organization and job design. In this context, workplace learning is likely to be a third-order strategy (Keep and Mayhew 1999). Workplaces are managed and organized to produce the goods and services, and their primary purpose is to make a profit. Similar priorities can be found in the public sector, where schools are organized to promote pupil rather than teacher learning and hospitals are organized to treat patients rather than to promote the learning of workers, even though the latter may be significant in delivering the service. This means that improvements to workers' learning always have to be balanced against other priorities.

Where companies do recognize the significance of learning for the enhancement of their HR, senior managers, acting as learning champions, may exert significant influence over the culture of an organization and its approach to supporting workplace learning. This will affect the expectations of managers, trainers, employees, and their representatives. Nevertheless, in large, complex organizations, translating expectations set at corporate level into practice may be more difficult. For example, Munro's case studies of Clover Unit and Arrow Unit within the same hospital, demonstrate that within the same organization, similar units may have very different cultures of learning. In Clover Unit, training was limited to health and safety and specialist courses, whereas Arrow Unit supported multidisciplinary team-working, producing a more expansive work environment as well as access to educational and job progression. Similarly, differences were observed between departments in Hodkinson and Hodkinson's studies of school teachers. Different departments within the same school had different approaches to cooperation and the sharing of information. Later in this chapter, we identify a number of ways in which actors at workplace level can seek to enhance learning opportunities.

At the lowest level, the past experiences and dispositions of individual workers will affect the extent to which they take advantage of the opportunities afforded by their immediate work environment. These are not fixed but can change over time. We know from research evidence that professionals and other highly qualified workers are more likely to have access to continuing training and professional development than less-qualified workers. They are also more likely to experience learning opportunities through the nature of the work environment and opportunities for boundary-crossing, than workers in lower-level jobs. The challenge is to create the conditions in which all workers can take advantage of these opportunities. One mechanism may be through entitlements to learning, established in law, through collective bargaining, or through the interventions of enlightened managers, trade unionists, trainers, and co-workers. Another mechanism is to build worker confidence through the recognition of tacit skills, as discussed by Evans and Kersh in Chapter 4. Examples of ways in which individual dispositions may be enhanced are also discussed in this conclusion.

Much of the existing literature on workplace learning tends to concentrate on one or at the most two of these scales, but struggles to pay due heed to all three. Thus, much of the work on communities of practice focuses on the immediate work setting or group and is not located in an understanding of the wider institutional context. Although its strengths lie in understanding learning as participation in the social relations of the workplace, it does not conceptualize the employment relationship, as we highlighted in Chapter 1, as a relationship that is contradictory and antagonistic. As Edwards argues, it is contradictory "because managements have to pursue the objectives of control and releasing creativity, both of which are inherent in the relationship with workers and which call for different approaches" (Edwards 2003: 16). Similarly, earlier work on reflective practice tended to focus mainly on the individual worker/learner. Activity theory, especially of the type developed by Engeström (2001) attempts to link local working practices with wider organizational frameworks. However, it takes the wider regulatory framework of Finnish social democracy, which underpins the relationship between managers and workers, for granted, and pays relatively little attention to individuals. There is much of value in all these approaches, but in what follows, we set out an alternative, holistic, and relational approach to improving workplace learning.

## The context of learning

We have stressed the interrelations between the different levels of the context in which workplace learning occurs. We have identified the role of social institutions in providing a more or less supportive structure for VET in formal educational institutions. Social institutions (and not just those governing VET), in turn, influence the more immediate context of the organization, contributing to a learning environment that can be characterized on the expansive–restrictive continuum in the workplace itself. This multilevel analysis has parallels with Whitley's (2000) concept of the social structuring of business systems, whereby work systems in different countries are characterized by

> contrasting ways of structuring tasks and jobs, of controlling how work is allocated, performed and rewarded, and of structuring employment relationships [. . .] these systems are linked to the nature of firms, interest groups, and dominant governance principles or "rules of the game" in different societies, which in turn stem from different patterns of industrialization.
>
> (2000: 88)

Whitley argues that radical transformation of the prevalent system in any society will be limited by the extent to which work-system characteristics are integrated with institutional arrangements (2000: 114).

This is not to argue that governments cannot intervene to enhance workplace learning. One recent development which may have the potential to enhance workplace learning in the UK is the statutory right established by the 2002 Employment Act for union learning representatives to have time off to perform their duties. This right was introduced in April 2003, and although many trade unions were developing policy and practice toward workplace learning prior to its introduction, our research does not allow us to evaluate its effects. This development has the potential to encourage trade unions to make training, development, and rights to learning more central to union concerns, whether they are pursued through the traditional collective bargaining agenda or through joint approaches with the employer. The involvement of trade unions may make some learning more appealing to workers, who have had little access to it in the past, by providing a support in a safe environment.

Nevertheless, there are a number of weaknesses in the legislation that mean that its capacity to promote workplace learning is limited.

First, there are no requirements on the employer to cooperate with trade unions on training, over and above the provision of leave for union learning-representative activities. Second, the objective of the legislation was always seen by government as raising workers' demand for learning (Rainbird 2005c). It does not provide employees with an entitlement to paid educational leave, and employers have no responsibility to work jointly with their representatives to enhance workplace learning. As such, it falls far short of the mechanisms in place in other EU member states, which encourage joint approaches to training and innovation at company level. Moreover, encouraged by the approach adopted by the Trades Union Congress, many trade unions concentrate on providing guidance and better access related to studying external courses, because this is what the legislation allows them to do. If the potential of the learning representatives movement is to be realized, learning representatives, managers, and trainers would need to work together to address issues relating to the workplace learning environment much more directly.

Less beneficial government interventions directly targeted at workplace learning include the NVQ system, which has been critiqued earlier in this book in Chapters 6 and 7. The extent to which this juggernaut has expanded or restricted learning environments is a matter for debate, and may partly depend upon local circumstances. Arguably, the huge investment in money, time, and people could have been better used in other ways. In the public sector, there are many examples of changes that impacted upon workplace learning environments, even though that was not their purpose. Thus, frequent changes in educational policy, national curriculum, assessment, and inspection regulations, resulted in both positive learning opportunities in schools, and negative factors such as increased stress and a lack of time to consolidate any partly learned new approaches. The increasing dominance of audit and measurable learning outcomes to meet short-term Treasury targets has skewed and distorted the types of learning that are possible in many public-sector workplaces.

## Constructing more expansive learning environments

This section addresses the extent to which more expansive learning environments can be created in the workplace. It could be argued that employers might find it easier to do this at times of relative prosperity than in times of contraction. Nevertheless, prosperity is not necessarily supportive of innovation and the reassessment of approaches to learning. Major investments in learning and the introduction of new forms of work organization are often introduced at times of crisis (Ashton and Sung 2002, Rainbird et al. 2003). It is at these times of crisis that employers may be prepared to contemplate innovative approaches to learning, including joint approaches with employee representatives, because the scale of change requires a high level of trust to reassure employees that their jobs and livelihoods are not under threat.

In the UK, there are no social institutions embedding cooperative approaches to learning at work. As a result, such developments have been dependent on the activities of "local enthusiastic actors" (Munro et al. 1997). At the level of the workplace, these might include managers, trainers, and trade-union representatives, who perceive the need to work together to enhance workplace learning. Innovation can also be costly and risky. Senker's analysis of the TCS in Chapter 5 demonstrates that introducing graduates into a company as change agents can produce significant innovation. Nevertheless, this is costly and, even where this is well supported by mentors within and outside the company, there is a risk of failure.

Organizational interventions are likely to be more effective under four conditions. These are:

1    Interventions need to address both employee and employer needs (Rainbird et al. 2003). Otherwise, it is possible to reduce the opportunities for learning and the effectiveness of learning, by making the learning environment more restrictive.
2    The involvement of employee representatives contributes to the expression of employees' interests and can reassure them that gains in productivity will not have a negative impact on jobs and conditions of employment (Rainbird et al. 2003).
3    Learning needs to be seen as an integral part of practice rather than a bolt-on activity. Interventions need to address the learning environment as a whole—for example, how both the work environment and formal learning can be made more expansive.
4    A short-term timeframe and a narrow view of learning, dominated by measurable changes in performance, will not enhance the learning environment and can stifle innovation.

The concept of a continuum of expansive and restrictive learning environments can be used as a tool to analyze and improve opportunities for learning, using a five-stage process. Drawing on our case-study materials, we identify a number of ways in which managers, trainers, trade unionists, and other practitioners can contribute to enhancing the workplace as a learning environment.

## Stage 1  Identify the dimensions of the existing learning environment

Using the approaches outlined in Chapter 2, and applied in Chapter 3, it is possible to analyze the dimensions of a learning environment using the expansive–restrictive continuum. The first step is to identify the relevant dimensions of the environment, each of which can be mapped between high restrictiveness and high expansiveness. The principle is that an expansive environment produces the widest opportunities for learning.

In identifying these dimensions, it is important to emphasize that even within one organization, the environments for different groups of workers will vary. So some occupational groups will experience an inherently more restrictive environment because of the way their jobs are designed. They may also experience limited opportunities for mobility into neighboring job territories or into more highly paid job roles, and this structures their access to training and career development. Even in occupations where there are job-progression ladders, some workers (women, members of ethnic minority groups) may experience greater barriers to promotion which, in turn, impact on their learning opportunities. Even within the same workplace, workers in the same occupation will have different experiences of the learning opportunities it affords.

Individual agency is also important: Workers co-construct the cultures where they work and they also co-construct the learning environment. In Hodkinson and Hodkinson's study of the school as a site of workplace learning (see Chapter 5), the cooperative dispositions of the music teachers and the more individualist approaches of the history teachers were significant in determining key dimensions of the learning environment in both departments.

It must be stressed that there is no simple formula or algorithm that can be used in all circumstances for identifying the dimensions of a learning environment. The perceptions of different actors will affect the extent to which potential changes in the local environment are perceived as an opportunity or a threat. In Chapter 2, Box 2.3 describes the introduction of changes in work organization and job design aimed at enhancing the learning environment for a specific group of workers in

Fuller and Unwin's Company C. Nevertheless, similar developments in job design (for example, the expansion of job roles through job rotation) may be experienced and interpreted in different ways, according to who initiates the changes and who is perceived to benefit from them (Munro and Rainbird 2002).

### Stage 2   Assess the current workplace against those dimensions

Once the dimensions of restriction and expansion have been identified, the next step is to identify the current position of the workplace or organization being analyzed against each dimension separately. This is not a matter of measurement or the application of scales. Rather, the opportunities and restrictions on learning need to be identified against that dimension. Thus, when collaboration was identified as a key dimension in school teacher learning, it was possible to examine the extent to which each department studied was cooperative. The resulting analysis showed that there was valuable cooperative learning in all four departments, but this was significantly stronger in two of them. This was because staff in the more cooperative departments routinely met in informal, nonwork time, such as the lunch hour. They often discussed ways of improving their teaching, shared ideas with each other, and intentionally learned from each other.

In any workplace, there are likely to be some dimensions that are more expansive, and others that are more restrictive. Extreme expansiveness on all dimensions is extremely unlikely and almost certainly undesirable. It is not unusual for two dimensions to pull in opposite directions. Maximizing opportunities for boundary-crossing, for example, might conflict with maximizing close within-team collaboration. Building new challenges into work can be beneficial for learning—but too many challenges can leave workers feeling demoralized and demotivated and may prevent new learning from being fully established before the next change comes along.

### Stage 3   Identify the potential for improvement

Once the current learning environment is assessed, the next step is to identify the possibilities for improvement. The most obvious way to do this is to examine the dimensions that are most restrictive and to work out what can be done to move them further toward expansion. This may not be either easy or straightforward. Job design may be extremely restrictive, and there may be limits to the extent to which it can be made more expansive.

The next problem is that making a dimension more expansive may entail changes that may require additional resources or changes to the way work is organized. Paid educational leave is an example of learning for employee need. Some employers may see it as contributing to an improvement in conditions of employment, providing workers with increased self-confidence and improved communication skills, reducing labor turnover and enhancing the adaptability of the workforce. For example, the Director of Personnel at East Coast NHS Trust, cited in Chapter 7, could point to improvements in team work and lower sickness and turnover rates as benefits of employee development, which were otherwise difficult to quantify in a systematic way. These benefits may be seen as compensating for the difficulties of managing cover and employee leave.

In the current managerial and economic climate in the UK, employers taking this perspective are in a minority. This is because many will perceive paid educational leave as increasing costs, as unnecessary for certain groups of workers, or that the money would be better spent on learning that was geared more closely to the employer's needs. This potentially desirable development would be more likely if there were legislation entitling workers to paid educational leave.

Managing paid educational leave is a key issue to be addressed in creating expansive learning environments. The difficulty of managing leave is a reason often cited by line managers for refusing to provide learning opportunities for frontline workers (UNISON, n.d.), yet they routinely manage sickness and holiday leave. Whereas managers and professional workers have considerable autonomy in managing their own workloads and can organize their time to allow for learning, this is not the case for many routine and manual workers. Fear of having to deal with more confident and empowered workers is one reason that may be behind managers' refusal to provide paid educational leave, and cover may be more effectively managed through economies of scale on an organization-wide basis than at the level of the individual unit (UNISON, n.d.).

### Stage 4  Identify the balance of advantage

Once the potential for improving the learning environment is known, the next stage is to determine which improvements make sense for the location or organization concerned. This will entail balancing the learning benefits from any such changes, against the ease with which such changes can be made and the effects of such changes on other priorities for the employer, trade-union members and other workers. As with so much of this work, there is no formula that can be applied in all situations. Different interest groups will have different perspectives on the costs and benefits of these developments.

Partly because of the complexity of these issues, and partly because of their contested nature, the eventual decisions about precisely how a particular learning environment can be improved will entail recognition of these different interests and whether mutual benefits can be identified.

### Stage 5  Implementation and monitoring

The implementation of changes to improve learning is a matter of specifics, and there is little we can add here. Once implemented, changes can and should be monitored. The key to success here is that monitoring should examine the changes to the learning environment as a whole, and their effects—on learning and other aspects of practice. For reasons explained elsewhere in the book, much of the improved learning that follows may not be directly measurable or identifiable as immediate outcomes.

## Workers' responses to their learning environment

Last but not least, workers themselves can sometimes make a difference, both for themselves and also for colleagues. It is a truism that those with higher-status positions and greater access to power are more able to do this than those with least. A cleaner working in isolation from other workers and with a restrictive work routine has much less scope to influence the learning environment than does a middle manager, school teacher, or hospital consultant. Different workers and groups of workers will react differently to the potential of their environment. This reemphasizes our initial assumption that conditions of employment are an important part of the learning environment itself. Issues such as work load, job satisfaction, hours of work, job security, promotion prospects, interesting challenges that are neither too great nor too frequent, supportive colleagues, trade-union support, and good management will all influence workers' dispositions to learn, as well as the opportunities themselves.

Where measures are introduced to make the workplace learning environment more expansive, they must not only increase the capacity for this environment to support learning, but must also increase individual's ability to take advantage of those opportunities in practice. The significance of workers' prior experience, dispositions, and identity was discussed in Chapters 4 and 5. This means that workers in the same organization may have different aspirations and will perceive the learning opportunities around them in different ways. For some, work is an important part of their lives and identity. For others, family, leisure, or voluntary work may be more important. Dispositions toward work and learning are also related to gender, ethnicity, social class, and age. It follows that the effective improvement of the learning environment at work should, as far as possible, take account of these dispositions, and be flexible in scope, allowing for and encouraging a range of possible reactions.

The first step toward such an integrated approach is to understand that making significant improvements to workplace learning has implications for the culture and practices of the workplace concerned. The difficulty is that if one or a small number of factors are changed, there may be knock-on effects on many others, some of which are difficult, if not impossible to predict. Equally, an apparently sensible and straightforward attempt to change a small group of factors may be undermined and rendered ineffective by the impact of others. In Chapter 4, we discussed how the head of a school history department tried to construct greater collegiality in the working of his department, to further enhance the mutual learning of all staff. Despite his attention to several significant factors, the patterns of work and learning remained largely unchanged.

The right to paid educational leave lies at the core of workers' entitlement to learning. Not only can paid educational leave provide workers with learning and job-progression opportunities, but the process of covering work can have wider pedagogical benefits as well, by providing work-experience opportunities. Moreover, the case study of Arrow Unit, discussed in Chapter 3, demonstrates that where workers progress into full-time study for professional qualifications in hospital settings, they can continue to provide cover for their colleagues.

Not all workers will want to take advantage of paid educational leave, and there will be a range of reasons for this. For those with basic skills needs, paid educational leave may draw attention to their weaknesses in a very public way (see Hoddinott 2000, for example). In contrast, Hodkinson and Hodkinson's research on school teacher learning identified that their learning could be improved by taking them out of their classrooms to work with teachers in other departments and schools. Yet school managers and the teachers themselves wanted to maximize the time spent in those classrooms, for the benefit of the pupils being taught.

The complex and integrated nature of workplace learning results in a possible paradox. On the one hand, we are trying to say things about improving workplace learning that apply across our varied research sites and across workplaces more generally. That is, we need to produce generalizable guidelines to the improvement of workplace learning. On the other hand, because so many different factors are involved and interrelated, the actual nature of workplace practice and workplace learning can look very different from one workplace to another, even within the same organization.

---

## Conclusion: Improving learning through facilitation, not control

The five-stage model for improving learning environments has been outlined in the earlier sections of this conclusion. In the final parts of the chapter, we need to reintroduce some further complications. The first is that interventions can be made at a variety of scales, together with the linked point that some interventions that make the greatest impact may not be directly aimed at improving learning at all.

In this book, we are advocating a dual-track approach which pays attention both to the context of learning and to the individual learner. This means improving the opportunities and incentives to learn at, for and through work, alongside measures targeted at workers as individuals. Our analysis and data support the view that where individual support is given, for example, though choices of course or in a mentoring scheme, this needs to form part of a wider strategy to enhance the workplace learning environment. The two alternative strategies, of environmental improvement and individual support, are not mutually exclusive. However, we would claim that the improvement of the learning environment is essential, if individually targeted approaches are to maximize their success.

In an age where universal top-down systems and solutions seem very popular, and where individual responsibility for learning is an almost universal mantra, this conclusion may seem controversial. We would simply reiterate two points already made. First, most workplace learning takes place informally through everyday working practices, and measures need to focus on enhancing the qualities of this broader environment. Second, even the best individualized approaches to learning improvement are only partially successful. These two facts represent realities that have to be dealt with, not ignored. Doing so offers more realistic opportunities to improve workplace learning. They are a source for hope, not for despair.

# Research methodology

## Aims and objectives

The Working to Learn (W2L) Network was funded as part of Phase I of the ESRC's Teaching and Learning Research Programme, a major national initiative to develop high-quality research that could contribute to the improvement of learning in a range of sectors and situations in the UK. As its title suggests, the W2L Network was focused on developing research that could help improve learning in workplaces. With this in mind, the Network had the following objectives:

- To develop an interdisciplinary understanding of the context of workplace learning, which is characterized by the conflict embodied in the wage relationship and wider systems for the management and regulation of employment.
- To explore and develop learning theory in relation to the pedagogy of the workplace.
- To test and refine contemporary theories of "apprenticeship" in a variety of contexts.
- To develop a better understanding of the practice of learning at, for, and through the workplace to the development of a concept of apprenticeship as a model of contemporary workplace teaching and learning.
- To build capacity in this underresearched field.
- To contribute to improved practice amongst a range of practitioners whose activities affect teaching and learning in the workplace and, in some cases, in formal educational contexts as well.

## The network approach

There were two distinctive features of the network methodology, and both related directly to the TLRP specification. The first was the involvement of practitioners, employers, and policy groups throughout the research process. This was a form of working that members of the group had used before, for example in the production of a report on improving the work-based route to learning for young people, for the then Institute of Personnel and Development (IPD) (Evans et al. 1997). This user engagement was achieved in several ways. The Network established an advisory group, with membership drawn from a range of work organizations, including employers, trade unions, the CIPD, and the Learning and Skills Development Agency (LSDA). This group contributed to the developing strategy of the Network, commented on interim findings, and helped in the dissemination process. The Network also employed Jim Sutherland, the former Director of Education and Training at UNISON, and Chair of the Government's Workplace Learning Task Group (1997–8) as a practitioner advisor. Jim was an integral part of the research team, helping to keep us focused on the needs of other practitioners and using his wide network of contacts to further inform the research. Next, each project run by the Network developed its own links with practitioners throughout the research process.

The nature of the research network itself was also distinctive. Rather than working as a team on one coordinated project, there were five small projects that made up the Network, each with its own small research team, and each with its own specific research focus. The five projects were as follows.

### Project 1   The regulatory framework of the employment relationship

This project was conducted by Helen Rainbird and Anne Munro. It was designed to provide the context for the other four projects. Cleaning and care were chosen to examine similar types of work and jobs under different regulatory frameworks. It built on earlier research on low-paid workers in the public sector conducted under the ESRC's Future of Work Programme. The researchers' theoretical position was based in a labor-process approach, giving particular attention to power relations in the workplace and their implications for learning opportunities.

Project 1 aimed to examine how the regulation of employment can influence opportunities for learning. This included:

- the relationship between pay structures and formal learning;
- the relationship between trade-union presence and access to training;
- the influence of national standards and statutory requirements on formal learning;
- the extent to which the workplace constitutes a community of practice and the opportunities provided for informal learning.

### Project 2   Recognition of tacit skills and knowledge in work reentry

This project was conducted by Karen Evans, with first Akiko Sakamoto and then Natasha Kersh. The project aimed to examine the limits of situated-learning theory, which has developed in ways that obscure the contributions of prior experiences and the effects of moving between contexts over time. Building on Evans's previous EU-funded work, 1998–2000, the underlying hypothesis was that, for those with interrupted work histories, tacit forms of personal competences are frequently underrecognized and underutilized in work reentry.

The project objectives were:

- to identify tacit forms of personal competences gained through the different configurations of life and work experiences of "adult returners" whose occupational biographies have been interrupted by family circumstances, unemployment, or changes of direction;
- to identify how, when, and under what circumstances recognition and deployment of "hidden capabilities" in learning and teaching situations strengthen learning success;
- to identify interrelationships between the recognition of tacit skills and student's/employee's learning processes and outcomes, as adults move between college and different workplace environments.

### Project 3   The workplace as a site for learning: Opportunities and barriers in SMEs

This project was conducted by Lorna Unwin and Alison Fuller. The project set out to examine the opportunities for and barriers to learning in SMEs, building on the researchers' existing studies of young people's experiences on the Modern Apprenticeship program. Drawing on social theories of learning, the project set out to articulate more clearly the ways in which workplace competence is attained through a combination of formal and informal learning. The setting for the project was the steel industry in England and Wales.

The overarching aim was to identify the factors influencing how inexperienced (apprentice) and experienced employees attain competence in the workplace. This was pursued through three objectives:

- examining the extent to which employees' skills, knowledge and competence map on to formal qualifications;
- problematizing the concept of "key skills" (mandatory for apprentices) in the workplace;
- examining broader organizational structures, job design, and workplace cultures within which learning environments are created and managed.

## Project 4  An exploration of the nature of apprenticeship as a site for learning in an advanced economy

This project was conducted by Peter Senker. The project built on his long-standing interest in engineering apprentices and the relevance of NVQ assessment to their learning. It also built on his research on the TCS, which employs young graduates, and his personal involvement in a voluntary organization providing respite care through carer-support workers (CSWs). The project aimed to:

- contribute to development of a theoretical model of "apprenticeship" in an advanced economy;
- explore this concept in three contexts: Modern Apprentices in engineering; TCS associates; and CSWs entering employment.

## Project 5  The school as a site for workplace learning

This project was conducted by Phil Hodkinson and Heather Hodkinson. The project grew out of their earlier research on the initial training of school teachers. This had demonstrated the significance of school and departmental cultures, which were explored here mainly in relation to the learning of experienced teachers. The project focused on three research questions:

1    What is the nature of teachers' informal learning and what is the relationship between informal and formal learning in teachers' professional development?
2    How does the culture of school and department influence the quality of the learning of teachers?
3    To what extent does helping teachers to understand their working cultures and the nature of their own informal learning enable them to improve their learning?

These projects were selected in order to provide different but overlapping perspectives on the objectives of the Network. The five projects were designed to generate empirical data from a range of contemporary settings that could be used to interrogate a number of influential theories and conceptual frameworks. These included situated learning, communities of practice, apprenticeship as a model of learning, informal learning, and tacit skills. The research included:

- young recruits, adult returners, and ongoing experienced workers;
- public and private sectors;
- occupations ranging from routine and manual jobs to professional occupations;
- predominantly male, predominantly female, and mixed-gender occupations.

In addition, each project developed from the particular interests and disciplinary backgrounds of the principal researchers involved. This maximized the varied expertise of the team, and meant that we could bring interdisciplinary perspectives to our analysis and theoretical development.

In effect, each project provided a different case study (or, more accurately, linked group of case studies). This focus on cases formed a central part of network methodology. This is because previous research shows that learning at work is significantly and directly influenced by the specific conditions, regulatory frameworks, and practices of particular workplaces. The multiple case-study approach recognized the truth. The variety of cases in the Network allowed us to identify the balance between specific factors and more generalizable influences.

The conduct of these case studies shared some common principles. All were concerned to study workplace learning through the detailed examination of normal working practices. We wanted to understand workplace learning through the perspectives of workers, managers, and, where relevant, trade-union officials. However, following other researchers in the field (for example, Beckett and Hager 2002, Billett 2001b, Eraut et al. 1998, Lave and Wenger 1991), we wanted to get beneath surface perceptions and understanding to explore more tacit practices and assumptions. In each case, we needed to understand workplace learning in relation to wider organizational structures and practices. This shared approach required each project to engage with detail and complexity. Given the limited resources, this required that case studies were small in scale and relatively few in number. It also required a predominantly qualitative approach to data collection, using interviews, observations, analysis of documentation, diaries, and a learning log, in one case supported by use of questionnaires.

In each project, data was collected over a period of time. For all except Project 2, data collection began in the autumn of 2000, and was completed in the autumn of 2003. Project 2 started and finished later, beginning data collection in spring 2001, and finishing in spring 2004. This longitudinal approach gave us the opportunity to develop an in-depth understanding of learning practice, of our research participants, and of the differing organizational contexts where we were studying it. It also allowed us to track changes in those contexts and practices and to engage with learning as an ongoing process. In all cases, data collection and analysis continued side by side, so that subsequent rounds of data collection were informed by what had already been discovered in earlier rounds.

In the course of the Network's research, interviews were conducted with 230 learners/employees of whom fifty-five were longitudinally tracked within or between sites of learning. A total of 170 questionnaires and 281 learning logs were completed by research participants. Ten colleges/training providers and forty-one workplace sites were researched, including private- and public-sector organizations, school departments, SMEs, service providers' sites, work placements, and TCS sites. Observations were carried out during more than 250 days of site visits, and interviews were conducted with 116 key informants (tutors, trainers, managers, employers, officers and representatives of trade-union and employer organizations, officers of sectoral training bodies).

Within this broad, shared network framework, each project developed its own specific methods, and they are described next.

## Individual project methodologies

### Project 1   The regulatory framework of the employment relationship

Eleven case studies were conducted of care and cleaning services in the public and private sectors, and in subcontractors to the public sector.

Data was collected through documents and interviews with senior managers, training managers, supervisors, union representatives where appropriate, between five and eight members of staff, and educational providers, in each case. Semi-structured schedules were used to investigate employment structure, strategic approaches to learning, adoption of standards, formal training, employee voice, work organization, and experiences of learning and assessment. Twelve case studies had been planned, but on the advice of our practitioners, the decision was made to conduct additional interviews with sectoral training bodies and national union officers and to include a private-sector provider of agency staff. To make this possible, we cut the number of cases to eleven.

A total of ninety-seven interviews were conducted. Some cleaning staff could not be released, so interviews were conducted as they worked. The pattern of access for the research mirrored the spaces available in working time for learning. In contrast to the intensity of cleaning work, in care homes there are pauses in activities around shift changeovers, used for training sessions and for sharing information about clients' needs.

This project had a small comparative element, involving Annette Jobert of Travail et Mobilités, Université Paris X, which explored the structures of collective bargaining and training in the cleaning industry in France. A series of joint meetings have taken place with her.

### Project 2   Recognition of tacit skills and knowledge in work reentry

Sixty-one adult learners following work reentry courses in social-care, management, and transport-sector jobs in six London region further/ adult education colleges were selected as research participants at the first stage of our research (beginning October 2000). The sample represented different degrees/types of interruption in occupational biographies of women and men. The second stage of research (beginning June 2002) involved detailed longitudinal tracking of selected cases into their workplaces or other destinations and reviewing with them what they had gained from their learning and how this is built upon after they move into new working environments. We aimed to follow up around 50 percent of the cases. While selecting cases (out of our sixty-one participants) to be followed up, we discovered that our original sample was reduced by about 20 percent as we had lost contact with a proportion of our respondents due to factors such as their change of accommodation, telephone numbers, or leaving the country. Some thirty cases to be longitudinally tracked into their workplaces or other destinations were chosen randomly from the rest of the sample (about 80 percent of our original sample).

Adults' learning experiences were researched through observations, semi-structured interviews with key informants (learners/trainers/supervisors/employers), questionnaires, and recordings of learning processes and achievements. The interviews with adult learners, including sixty-one initial interviews and thirty follow-up interviews, attempted to elicit a wide range of tacit skills by asking adult learners about their life and work experiences and relating these to their learning outcomes and achievements. Data collection also included semi-structured interviews with twenty tutors/training providers, twelve employers, and thirty self-completion learner questionnaires (to check consistency of interpretations) which were completed by a subsample, giving responses against a set of fixed indicators of skill development and use. Observations (of all sixty-one learners) were conducted in colleges of adult education with the objective to observe (1) the way the adult learners use and deploy their tacit skills and competences in their learning environments and (2) to what extent their skills are recognized by others (including their teachers/trainers, fellow learners).

Data collection used structured elicitation techniques (Eraut 1999) to identify tacit dimensions of personal competences of importance in the learning/work transitions of adults. Responses from interviewees have been analyzed with the assistance of a qualitative analysis software program, called "NVivo." The dynamic concept analysis (DCA) method has assisted in clarifying the interrelationships between learning and skill recognition in different environments and was further simplified for practitioner use. This DCA allows the analysis of data using conceptual models based on information about concept relations in adult learning (Kontiainen 2002, Evans et al. 2004). For this case study, we considered concepts (or variables) such as ability to work with others, managing conflicts skills, negotiation skills, involvement, ability to abide by rules and regulations, social interaction skills, and team-work skills. Each variable has three attributes such as *a* (high, good, or active), *n* (medium), and *b* (poor, low, or passive). The models show which of the attributes describe a single case study and specify relationships among the concepts. The method has subsequently been incorporated into the learning tasks to uncover and establish links and interrelationships between acquired or potential personal competences and certain learning activities. Further testing has continued to 2005 as some practitioners collaborating in the research have continued to work with the tools and approaches developed in the research.

### Project 3   The workplace as a site for learning: Opportunities and barriers in SMEs

This project used a multilevel and case-study methodology in order to examine the relationship between apprenticeship and the wider organizational context in which the apprentices were working and learning. The project team had previously conducted research in the UK steel industry, a sector that is undergoing significant restructuring due to the intense global competition for its products. This research had shown that the sector has an aging workforce and that it was struggling to attract young people due to its image as a "dirty" and dying industry. In addition, a major shift was taking place away from the large-scale plants that manufacture steel, toward much smaller businesses that transform steel into specialized products. It was decided, therefore, to site the project in the steel sector to see how apprenticeship was being used and developed in such dynamic circumstances. The researchers had existing links with the then Steel and Metals National Training Organization and approached the personnel responsible for managing the government-funded Modern Apprenticeship program throughout the UK. This connection proved to be vital in gaining access to companies to discuss whether they would be prepared to participate in the research. Meetings were held with a number of companies, four of whom were prepared to give the researchers the range of access they needed to pursue their objectives. The four companies were also felt to be representative of the changing face of the steel industry in that:

- one was an old-style manufacturer with a history of apprenticeship;
- one was a highly specialized business with no history of apprenticeship, but now employing apprentices as a way to recruit young people;

- one was a well-established manufacturer of steel products with a long history of apprenticeship that had recently changed from family ownership due to a takeover by a venture capital company;
- one was a stockholder, buying and selling steel bars and rods, and so employing a workforce of sales people and warehouse staff, and, which, like the second company, had only recently employed an apprentice for the first time.

The project used a range of methods to collect data, including tape-recorded individual and group interviews, observation of employees' workplace activity and of apprentices being assessed for competence-based qualifications, surveys of employee attitudes to learning at work, analysis of organizational documentation, and employee learning logs.

The learning log proved to be an innovative and effective method to help people reflect on and record their teaching and learning activities, both systematically and longitudinally. The log developed from the team's concern that, in interviews, individuals would remember some aspects of their workplace learning but the more "everyday" incidents might be overlooked. De-briefing interviews with people after completing the logs were necessary to learn more about how they had selected which items to record and overcome any misunderstandings. The methodological message drawn from the research was the importance of deploying a range of complementary data-collection techniques to open up the "closed box" of the phenomenon "learning at work." A sample of employees in all four companies were invited to complete a log on a weekly basis for a period of eight weeks. The researchers found that the logs were an effective catalyst for these interviews as the employees were often surprised at how much activity they had recorded in the different sections of the log. In particular, the section of the log that asked for details about whether an employee had helped a colleague at work to learn proved to be very illuminating in the case of the apprentices. This showed that apprentices were not only helping each other, but also their older and more experienced colleagues.

The sample for the interviews in each company was derived from the organizational structure in order to ensure that the perspective of people at all levels (from directors down to shopfloor workers) was obtained. In addition, where possible, company documentation relating to training and development policies was analyzed to see how far it aligned with the perspective being gathered in the interviews. In terms of fieldwork, the project carried out the following data-collection activities:

- sixty one-to-one interviews;
- thirteen group interviews;
- six observations;
- two "learning at work surveys" in two organizations covering 300 employees;
- 281 weekly learning logs completed by twenty-nine apprentices and older workers employed by the four companies.

A detailed report of the findings from the data collected was summarized for each case study site for use in consultative briefings to the research participants. Feedback from these briefings further informed the data analysis. The expansive–restrictive continuum, developed earlier in the project (and outlined in Chapter 2), was used as the main analytical framework for interpreting the data.

### Project 4   An exploration of the nature of apprenticeship as a site for learning in an advanced economy

This project was conducted in two stages. The research proposal defined new entrants to work as "apprentices," in that all new entrants into occupations could in a sense be described as "apprentices." Using semi-structured interviews, Stage 1 explored the appropriateness of this definition in terms of the relevance of the concepts developed by Lave and Wenger (1991) that apprenticeship represents peripheral participation in communities of practice, and that over time peripheral participants become "experts" in communities of practice. It compared the learning experiences of initial entrants to three very different occupations—advanced modern apprentices in mechanical engineering, TCS associates, and CSWs—who work and learn in very different contexts.

Stage 1 included interviews with "apprentices" in all three contexts (see Table A.1). The access strategy was built on the researcher's personal involvement in Caretree, the voluntary organization, and prior research contacts. This facilitated access to CSWs, their managers, and trainers. The project also built on two earlier studies for the TCD.

The methodology was adapted from Eraut's ESRC study (Eraut et al. 1998) which used a semi-structured checklist for learners. However, unlike the Eraut study, questions similar to those asked of learners were also asked of supervisors and trainers so as to secure a rounded and balanced picture of learning.

*Table A.1*  Stage 1 interviews

| Sector | Learners | Training managers/company supervisors/managers |
|---|---|---|
| Modern Apprentices | 3 | 3 |
| TCS associates | 4 | 4 |
| CSWs | 4 | 1 |
| Total | 11 | 8 |

Principally because in a small project it was advisable to concentrate resources on two rather than three areas, it was agreed that Project 4 should omit modern apprentices from the next stage of the research, and further interviews were undertaken (see Table A.2).

*Table A.2*  Stage 2 interviews

| Sector | Learners | Company supervisors/ academic supervisors/ managers |
|---|---|---|
| TCS associates | 9 | 16 |
| CSWs | 12 | 11 |
| Total | 21 | 27 |

## Project 5  The school as a site for workplace learning

In looking at the school as a site for workplace learning for teachers, we carried out longitudinal case studies between 2000 and 2003 of the teachers in four subject departments of two English secondary schools. Both schools took pupils from the age of eleven to eighteen years, but one had a rural catchment and the other a mixed catchment within a major city. The departments were history, music, art, and IT. These departments were selected because they were small enough for us to interview and to observe all teachers within them, thus avoiding further sampling difficulties. Access had to be negotiated with the school and the teachers concerned. As a result, all four were departments where teaching was judged to be strong.

The data collected included

- documentary evidence from national bodies, schools, departments, and individual teachers on staff development and learning matters;
- observation within the schools, and particularly of the teachers working in their departments;
- up to three semi-structured interviews with each teacher about their career history and learning as a teacher.

Nineteen teachers, four student teachers and two senior teachers were directly involved in the research. There were fifty-five transcribed interviews and fifty-one days of observation. Fieldwork extended over six school terms (two years) with alternate terms being spent in each school. We also held meetings with the schools to seek feedback about emerging findings, halfway through the research and near the end. Data were analyzed cyclically, so that subsequent collection sweeps were informed by previous findings, as well as by insights from the other network projects. Data was visited and revisited in the light of developing ideas and theory. At each stage, the analysis was heuristic (Moustakas 1990) and interpretative (Wolcott 1994). We worked by immersing ourselves in the data and by constructing detailed pictures and narratives of individual teachers' learning and of the cultures and practices of each department. Finally, we considered the data holistically.

## Synthesizing the findings

The Network was managed and administrated from Northampton. Charlotte Spokes, the Research Administrator, was responsible for day-to-day coordination between the team and their respective institutions. The Network Team was integrated through regular two-day residential meetings, backed up by regular email and telephone contacts. Some of these meetings were followed by advisory-group meetings. Links with the academic community were developed through a two-day international conference and two workshops, jointly run with the ESRC's designated research centre, SKOPE (Skills, Knowledge and Organizational Performance).

The internal and external network links facilitated the progressive synergizing of the findings. In the early stages of the research, this focused on sharing methodological ideas and issues arising from early data. Even at this stage, regular meetings allowed a creative exchange of ideas, as we each learned from the approaches and thinking of the others.

As time progressed, findings became more substantial. We used brainstorming approaches to identify a wide range of issues arising across the projects and looked for ways to group them. We also tested out ideas that were emerging from one project to see how relevant they were in the others. Because this process began well before fieldwork had finished, fieldwork could be progressively refined to focus on such relevant ideas.

Over time, we focused on three interlocking themes, which form the substantive material in this book. The development of each theme was led by a group of the research team, with everyone leading on one of them. In addition, we each developed the themes in relation to our own data, and used that project data to further refine and construct the theme development. All projects contributed to each of the themes, but in different ways, depending upon their specific findings. The three themes were presented as working papers in a joint workshop with SKOPE, which helped further refine our thinking. The interrelationships between the themes were then developed, as were the implications for improving workplace learning.

This integration has resulted in findings and theoretical understandings that transcend individual projects. As is to be expected in such a large and diverse team, differences of emphasis and of theoretical preference still remain, and each project, taken individually, stands as a significant contribution to the field in its own right.

## Conclusion

The findings, analysis, and theorizing within this research network are underpinned and substantiated by the methodology used. In particular, the range and variety of our sample case studies give us confidence in the wider applicability of our approach in many different workplace contexts. Those case studies are each based upon detailed and comprehensive data, drawn from a variety of sources and using a variety of methods. The different disciplinary backgrounds and interests of the research team, and the fact that the major findings are common to us all, further validates the analysis. The involvement of a wide range of different practitioners and policymakers in all stages of the research helped ensure that our synthesis remained relevant and accessible to nonresearchers.

Finally, findings were exposed and refined through "live peer review" by practitioners and academic researchers in the field, at conferences, seminars, and workshops.

# Bibliography

Alheit, P. and Dausien, B. (2002) "The Double Face of Lifelong Learning: Two Analytical Perspectives in a 'Silent Revolution,'" *Studies in the Education of Adults*, 34 (1): 3–22.

Antikainen, A., Houtsonen, J., Kauppila, J., and Huotelin, H. (1996) *Living in a Learning Society: Life Histories, Identities and Education*, London: Falmer.

Appelbaum, E. and Batt, R. (1994) *The New American Workplace: Transforming Work Systems in the United States*, London: ILR Press.

Appelbaum, E., Bailey, T., Berg, P., and Kalleberg, A. L. (2000) *Manufacturing Advantage: Why High-Performance Work Systems Pay Off*, London: Cornell University Press.

Armstrong, P. F. (1987) "Qualitative Strategies in Social and Educational Research: The Life History Method in Theory and Practice," *Newland Papers 14*, Hull: University of Hull.

Ashton, D. (2004) "The Political Economy of Workplace Learning," in H. Rainbird et al. (eds) *Workplace Learning in Context*, London: Routledge, pp. 21–37.

Ashton, D. and Sung, J. (2002) *Supporting Workplace for High Performance Working*, Geneva: International Labour Office.

Barnett, R. (1994) *The Limits of Competence*, Buckingham: OU/SRHE Press.

—— (2004) *The Limits of Competence*, Buckingham: SRHE/Open University Press.

Bateson, G. (1972) *Steps to an Ecology of Mind*, New York: Balantine Books.

Beckett, D. and Hager, P. (2002) *Life, Work and Learning: Practice in Postmodernity*, London: Routledge.

Beinart, S. and Smith, P. (1998) *National Adult Learning Survey*, Research Report 49, Nottingham: Department for Education and Employment.

Biemans, H., Nieuwenhuis, L., Poell, R., Mulder, M. and Wesselink, R. (2004) "Competence-Based VET in the Netherlands: Background and Pitfalls," *Journal of Vocational Education and Training*, 56 (4): 523–38.

Billett, S. (1998) "Constructing Vocational Knowledge: Situations and Other Social Sources," *Journal of Education and Work*, 11 (3): 255–73.

—— (2001a) "Learning through Working Life: Interdependencies at Work," *Studies in Continuing Education*, 23 (1): 19–35.

—— (2001b) *Learning in the Workplace: Strategies for Effective Practice*, Crows Nest, NSW: Allen & Unwin.

—— (2002) "Critiquing Workplace Learning Discourses: Participation and Continuity at Work," *Studies in the Education of Adults*, 34 (1): 56–67.

—— (2004) "Learning through Work: Workplace Participatory Practices," in H. Rainbird et al. (eds) *Workplace Learning in Context*, London: Routledge.

Billett, S. and Somerville, M. (2004) "Transformations at Work: Identity and Learning," *Studies in Continuing Education*, 26 (2): 309–26.

Billett, S., Barker, M. and Hernon-Tinning, B. (2004) "Participatory Practices at Work," *Pedagogy, Culture and Society*, 12 (2): 233–57.

Black, H. and Wolf, A. (eds) *Knowledge and Competence*, London: Careers and Occupational Information Centre/HMSO.

Boreham, N., Samurcay, R., and Fischer, M. (eds) (2002) *Work Process Knowledge*, London: Routledge.

Boud, D. and Garrick, J. (eds) (1999) *Understanding Learning at Work*, London: Routledge.

Boud, D. and Solomon, N. (eds) (2001) *Work-Based Learning: A New Higher Education?* Buckingham: Open University/SRHE Press.

—— (2003) "I Don't Think I Am a Learner: Acts of Naming Learners at Work," *Journal of Workplace Learning*, 15 (7/8): 326–31.

Bourdieu, P. (1984) *Distinction: A Social Critique of the Judgement of Taste*, London: Routledge & Kegan Paul.

Bourdieu, P. and Wacquant, L. J. D. (1992) *An Invitation to Reflexive Sociology*, Cambridge: Polity Press.

British Cleaning Council (2003) Online. Available HTTP: <http://www.britishcleaningcouncil.org> (accessed 10 November 2003).

Brown, A. and Keep, E. (1999) *Review of Vocational Education and Training Research in the United Kingdom*, Brussels: European Commission.

Brown, J. S., Collins, A., and Duguid, P. (1989) "Situated Cognition and the Culture of Learning," *Educational Researcher*, 18 (1): 32–42.

Cleaning Industry National Training Organization (CINTO) (2001) *Cleaning Industry Sector Workforce Development Plan 2001–2003*, Northampton: CINTO.

Coffield, F. (2000) *Differing Visions of a Learning Society*, Bristol: Policy Press.

—— (ed.) (2000) *The Necessity of Informal Learning*, Bristol: Policy Press in association with the ESRC Learning Society Programme.

Colling, T. (2000) "Personnel Management in the Extended Organization," in S. Bach and K. Sisson (eds) *Personnel Management in Britain: A Comprehensive Guide to Theory and Practice*, Oxford: Blackwell.

Commission for Social Care Inspection (2004) *Inspecting for Better Lives: Modernizing the Regulation of Social Care*, Newcastle: CSCI.

Confederation of British Industry (CBI) and Trades Union Congress (TUC) (2001) *Skills for Productivity and Employability: Submission to the Productivity Initiative*, London: Confederation of British Industry and Trades Union Congress.

Cross, K. P. (1981) *Adults as Learners*, San Francisco, Calif.: Jossey-Bass.

Crouch, C. (2000) *Coping with Post-Democracy*, London: Fabian Society.

Crouch, C. and Streeck, W. (1997) (eds) *Political Economy of Modern Capitalism*, London: Sage.

Darrah, C. N. (1996) *Learning and Work: An Exploration in Industrial Ethnography*, New York: Garland.

Davey, J. (2003) "Opportunity or Outrage? Redundancy and Educational Involvement in Mid-Life," *Journal of Education and Work*, 16 (1): 87–102.

Department of Health (DoH) (2003) *Domiciliary Care, National Minimum Standards*, London: Department of Health Publications.

—— (2004) *Matron's Charter: An Action Plan for Cleaner Hospitals*, London: Department of Health Publications.

Department for Education and Employment (DfEE) (1998) *The Learning Age: A New Renaissance for a New Britain*, Norwich: HMSO.

Department for Education and Skills (DfES) (2003) *21st Century Skills. Realizing Our Potential. Individuals, Employers, Nation*. Cm 5810, London: The Stationery Office.

Edwards, P. (ed.) (2003) *Industrial Relations: Theory and Practice*, 2nd edn, Oxford: Blackwell.

Employment Department (ED) (1988) *Employment for the 1990s*, Norwich: HMSO.

Engeström, Y. (1994) *Training for Change: New Approach to Instruction and Learning in Workplace Life*, Geneva: International Labour Office.

—— (1996a) "Innovative Learning in Work Teams: Analyzing Cycles of Knowledge Creation in Practice," in Y. Engeström, R. Miettinen and R. Punamiki (eds) (1999) *Perspectives on Activity Theory*, Cambridge: Cambridge University Press.

—— (1996b) "The Tensions of Judging: Handling Cases of Driving under the Influence of Alcohol in Finland and Canada," in Y. Engeström and D. Middleton (eds) *Cognition and Communication at Work*, Cambridge: Cambridge University Press.

—— (1999) "Activity Theory and Individual and Social Transformation," in Y. Engeström., R. Miettinen, and R. Punamiki (eds) (1999) *Perspectives on Activity Theory*, Cambridge: Cambridge University Press.

—— (2001) "Expansive Learning at Work: Towards an Activity-Theoretical Reconceptualization," *Journal of Education and Work*, 14 (1): 133–56.

—— (2004) "The New Generation of Expertise: Seven Theses," in H. Rainbird, A. Fuller, and A. Munro (eds) *Workplace Learning in Context*, London: Routledge.

Engeström, Y., Engeström, R., and Karkkainen, M. (1995) "Polycontextuality and Boundary Crossing in Expert Cognition: Learning and Problem-Solving in Complex Work Activities," *Learning and Instruction*, 5 (1): 319–66.

Engeström, Y., Miettinen, R., and Punamaki, R. (eds) (1999) *Perspectives on Activity Theory*, Cambridge: Cambridge University Press.

Eraut, M. (1999) "Theoretical and Methodological Perspectives on Researching Workplace Learning," American Educational Research Association Conference, Montreal.

—— (2000) "Non-Formal Learning, Implicit Learning and Tacit Knowledge," in F. Coffield (ed.) *The Necessity of Informal Learning*, Bristol: Policy Press in association with the ESRC Learning Society Programme.

—— (2004) "Transfer of Knowledge between Education and Workplace Settings," in H. Rainbird, A. Fuller, and A. Munro, *Workplace Learning in Context*, London: Routledge.

Eraut, M., Alderton, J., Cole, G., and Senker, P. (1998a) *Development of Knowledge and Skills in Employment*, Falmer: University of Sussex Institute of Education.

—— (1998b) "Learning from Other People at Work," in F. Coffield, (ed.) *Learning at Work*, Bristol: Policy Press.

—— (2000) "Development of Knowledge and Skills at Work," in F. Coffield (ed.) *Differing Visions of a Learning Society*, Research Findings, Vol. I, Bristol: Policy Press.

Eraut, M., Steadman, S., Trill, J., and Parkes, J. (1996) *The Assessment of NVQs*, Research Report No. 4, University of Sussex: Institute of Education.

European Commission (2001) *Making a European Area of Lifelong Learning*, Luxembourg: Office for Official Publications of the European Communities.

Evans, K. (2002a) "Taking Control of their Lives?" *Journal of Youth Studies*, 5 (3): 245–69.

—— (2002b) "The Challenges of 'Making Learning Visible': Problems and Issues in Recognizing Tacit Skills and Key Competences," in K. Evans et al. (eds) *Working to Learn: Transforming Learning in the Workplace*, London: Kogan Page, pp. 29–43.

—— (2002c) "Continuing Professional Development," in L. Gearon (ed.) *Education in the United Kingdom: Structures and Organisation*, London: David Fulton.

—— (2005) "Tacit Skills and Occupational Mobility in a Global Culture," in J. Zajda (ed.) *The International Handbook on Globalization, Education and Policy Research*, Dordrecht: Springer.

Evans, K. and Kersh, N. (2004) "Recognition of Tacit Skills and Knowledge: Sustaining Learning Outcomes in Workplace Environments," *Journal of Workplace Learning*, 16 (1): 63–74.

Evans, K. and Niemeyer, B. (2004) *Reconnection: Countering Social Exclusion through Situated Learning*, Dordrecht: Kluwer/Springer.

Evans, K. and Rainbird, H. (2002) "The Significance of Workplace Learning for a Learning Society," in K. Evans, P. Hodkinson, and L. Unwin (eds)

*Working to Learn: Transforming Learning in the Workplace*, London: Routledge.

Evans, K., Hodkinson, P., and Unwin, L. (eds) (2002) *Working to Learn: Transforming Learning in the Workplace*, London: Routledge.

Evans, K., Kersh, N., and Kontiainen, S. (2004a) "Recognition of Tacit Skills: Sustaining Learning Outcomes in Adult Learning and Work Re-Entry," *International Journal of Training and Development*, 8 (1): 54–72.

Evans, K., Kersh, N., and Sakamoto, A. (2004b) "Learner Biographies: Exploring Tacit Dimensions of Knowledge and Skills," in H. Rainbird, A. Fuller, and A. Munro (eds) *Workplace Learning in Context*, London: Routledge.

Evans, K., Hodkinson, P., Keep, E., Maguire, M., Raffe, D., Rainbird, H., Senker, P., and Unwin, L. (1997) *Working to Learn*, London: Chartered Institute of Personnel and Development.

Finegold, D. and Soskice, D. (1988) "The Failure of Training in Britain: Analysis and Prescription," *Oxford Review of Economic Policy*, 4 (3): 21–53.

Finn, D. (1987) *Training without Jobs: New Deals and Broken Promises*, Basingstoke and London: Macmillan Education.

Fox, A. (1966) *Industrial Sociology and Industrial Relations*, London: HMSO.

Fuller, A. and Unwin, L. (1998) "Reconceptualising Apprenticeship: Exploring the Relationship between Work and Learning," *Journal of Vocational Education and Training*, 50 (2): 153–71.

—— (2002) "Developing Pedagogies for the Contemporary Workplace," in K. Evans, P. Hodkinson, and L. Unwin (eds) *Working to Learn: Transforming Learning in the Workplace*, London: Routledge.

—— (2003a) "Learning as Apprentices in the Contemporary UK Workplace: Creating and Managing Expansive and Restrictive Participation," *Journal of Education and Work*, 16 (4): 407–26.

—— (2003b) "Creating a 'Modern Apprenticeship': A Critique of the UK's Multi-Sector, Social Inclusion Approach," *Journal of Education and Work*, 16 (1): 5–25.

—— (2004a) "Expansive Learning Environments: Integrating Personal and Organizational Development," in H. Rainbird et al. (eds) *Workplace Learning in Context*, London and New York: Routledge.

—— (2004b) "Young People as Teachers and Learners in the Workplace: Challenging the Novice-Expert Dichotomy," *International Journal of Training and Development*, 8 (1): 31–41.

—— (2005) "Older and Wiser? Workplace Learning from the Perspective of Experienced Employees," *International Journal of Lifelong Education*, 24 (1): 21–39.

Fuller, A., Hodkinson, H., Hodkinson, P., and Unwin, L. (2005) "Learning as Peripheral Participation in Communities of Practice: A Reassessment of Key Concepts in Workplace Learning," *British Educational Research Journal*, 31 (1): 49–68.

Fuller, A., Ashton, D., Felstead, A., Unwin, L., Walters, S., and Quinn, M. (2003) *The Impact of Informal Learning at Work on Business Productivity*, London: Department of Trade and Industry.

Geary, J. (1995) "Work Practices: The Structure of Work," in P. Edwards (ed.) *Industrial Relations: Theory and Practice*, Oxford: Blackwell.

Gehin, J.-P. and Jobert, A. (2001) "International Briefing 8: Training and Development in France," *International Journal of Training and Development*, 5 (1): 81–90.

Giddens, A. (1991) *Modernity and Self-Identity: Self and Society in the Late Modern Age*, Cambridge: Polity Press.

Goodson, I. F. (2004) "All the Lonely People: Education and the Struggle for Private Meaning and Public Purpose," University of Brighton, Inaugural Lecture, November 9.

Green, F. (1999) "Training the Workers," in P. Gregg and J. Wandsworth (eds) *The State of Working Britain*, Manchester: Manchester University Press.

Grugulis, I. (2003) "National Vocational Qualifications: A Research-Based Critique," British *Journal of Industrial Relations*, 41 (3): 457–75.

Grugulis, I., Vincent, S., and Hebson, G. (2003) "The Rise of the 'Network Form' and the Decline of Discretion," *Human Resource Management Journal*, 13 (2): 45–59.

Guile, D. (2005) *Work-Based Learning Explained*: *Centre for Excellence in Work-Based Learning for Education Professionals*, London: Institute of Education.

Guile, D. and Young, M. (1995) "Further Professional Development and FE Teachers: Setting an New Agenda for Work-Based Learning," in I. Woodward (ed.) *Continuing Professional Development Issues in Design and Delivery*, London: Cassell, pp. 235–68.

Hager, P. (2004) "The Competence Affair, or Why Vocational Education and Training Urgently Needs a New Understanding of Learning," *Journal of Vocational Education and Training*, 56 (3): 409–33.

Hall, P. and Soskice, D. (eds) (2001) *Varieties of Capitalism: The Institutional Foundations of Comparative Advantage*, Oxford: Oxford University Press.

Harris, H. (2000) *Defining the Future or Reliving the Past? Unions, Employers, and the Challenge of Workplace Learning*, Information Series No. 380. Columbus, Ohio: ERIC Clearing House on Adult, Career, and Vocational Education.

Harzing, A.-V. and Van Ruysseveldt, J. (eds) (2004) *International Human Resource Management*, 2nd edn, London: Sage.

Heidegger, G. (1997) "The Social Shaping of Work and Technology as a Guideline for Vocational Education and Training," *Journal of European Industrial Training* 2 (6/7): 238–74.

Helsby, G. (1999) *Changing Teachers' Work*, Buckingham: Open University Press.

Hoddinott, S. (2000) "The Worker Basic Skills Crisis: Some Industrial Relations Implications," in H. Rainbird (ed.) *Training in the Workplace: Critical Perspectives on Learning at Work*, Basingstoke: Macmillan.

Hodkinson, P. (1996) "Careership: The Individual, Choices and Markets in the Transition into Work," in J. Avis et al. (eds) *Knowledge and Nationhood: Education, Politics and Work*, London: Cassell.

Hodkinson, P. and Bloomer, M. (2002) "Learning Careers: Conceptualizing Lifelong Work-Based Learning," in K. Evans, P. Hodkinson and L. Unwin (eds) *Working to Learn: Transforming Learning in the Workplace*, London: Kogan Page.

Hodkinson, P. and Hodkinson, H. (2003) "Individuals, Communities of Practice and the Policy Context: School-Teachers Learning in their Workplace," *Studies in Continuing Education*, 25 (1): 3–21.

—— (2004a) "The Significance of Individuals' Dispositions in Workplace Learning: A Case Study of Two Teachers," *Journal of Education and Work*, 17 (2): 167–82.

—— (2004b) "Rethinking the Concept of Community of Practice in Relation to Schoolteachers' Workplace Learning," *International Journal of Training and Development*, 8 (1): 21–31.

Hodkinson, P. and Issitt, M. (1995) *The Challenge of Competence: Professionalism through Vocational Education and Training*, London: Cassell.

Hodkinson, P., Sparkes, A. C., and Hodkinson, H. (1996) *Triumphs and Tears: Young People, Markets and the Transition from School to Work*, London: David Fulton.

Hodkinson, P., Hodkinson, H., Evans, K. and Kersh, N., with A. Fuller, L. Unwin, and P. Senker (2004) "The Significance of Individual Biography in Workplace Learning," *Studies in the Education of Adults*, 36 (1): 6–26.

Hodkinson, P., Anderson, G., Colley, H., Davies, J., Diment, K., Scaife, T., Tedder, M., Wahlberg, M., and Wheeler, E. (2004) "Learning Cultures in Further Education," British Educational Research Association Annual Conference, UMIST, Manchester.

Huys, R. and Hootegem, G. V. (2002) "A Delayed Transformation? Changes in the Division of Labour and their Implications for Learning Opportunities," in N. Boreham, R. Samurcay, and M. Fischer (eds) *Work Process Knowledge*, London: Kogan Page.

Hyland, T. (1994) *Competence, Education and NVQs: Dissenting Perspectives*, London: Cassell.

Hyman, R. and Streeck, W. (eds) (1988) *New Technology and Industrial Relations*, Oxford: Blackwell.

Illeris, K. (2004) *Adult Education and Adult Learning*, Malabar, Fla.: Krieger Publishing Company.

Issitt, M. (1995) "Competence, Professionalism and Equal Opportunities," in P. Hodkinson and M. Issitt (eds) *The Challenge of Competence*, London: Cassell Education.

James, D. and Diment, K. (2003) "Going Underground? Learning and Assessment in an Ambiguous Space," *Journal of Vocational Education and Training*, 55 (4): 407–22.

Johnson, B. and Lundvall, B.-A. (2001) "Why all this Fuss about Codified and Tacit Knowledge?" DRUID International Conference, Aalborg.

Jordon, B. (1991) "Competencies and Values," *Social Work Education*, 10 (1): 5–11.

Jorgenson, C. H. and Warring, N. (2002) "Learning in the Workplace: The Interplay between Learning Environments and Biography," ESREA Conference on Adult Education and the Labour Market VII, Roskilde University, May 30–June 1.

Kelly, A. (2001) "The Evolution of Key Skills: Towards a Tawney Paradigm," *Journal of Vocational Education and Training*, 53 (1): 21–35.

Keep, E. (1994) "Vocational Education and Training for the Young," in K. Sisson (ed.) *Personnel Management: A Comprehensive Guide to Theory and Practice in Britain.* Oxford: Blackwell, pp. 299–333.

—— (2002) "Creating a Knowledge Driven Economy: Definitions, Challenges and Opportunities," SKOPE Policy Paper No. 2, Universities of Oxford and Warwick.

—— (2004) "The State and Power: An Elephant and a Snake in the Telephone Box of English VET Policy," unpublished paper, University of Warwick, ESRC Centre on Skills, Knowledge and Organizational Performance.

Keep, E. and Mayhew, K. (1988) "The Assessment: Education, Training and Economic Performance," *Oxford Review of Economic Policy*, 4 (3): i–xv.

—— (1999) "The Assessment: Knowledge, Skills and Competitiveness," *Oxford Review of Economic Policy*, 15 (1): 1–15.

Keep, E. and Rainbird, H. (2000) "Towards the Learning Organization?," in S. Bach and K. Sisson (eds) *Personnel Management: A Comprehensive Guide to Theory and Practice*, 3rd edn, Oxford: Blackwell, pp. 173–94.

Kemshall, H. (1993) "Assessing Competence: Scientific Process or Subjective Interference? Do We Really See It?," *Social Work Education*, 12 (1): 36–45.

Kennedy, H. (1995) *Return to Learn: Unison's Fresh Approach to Trade Union Education*, London: Unison.

Kern, H. and Schumann, M. (1984) *Des Ende des Facharbeiteraufstiegs? Neue mittlere Bildungs: Und Karrierewege in Deutschland und Frankreich, ein Vergleic*, Frankfurt and New York: Beck.

Kersh, N. and Evans, K. (2005) "Self-Evaluation of Tacit Skills and Competences of Adult Learners," *European Education*, 37 (2): 87–98.

King, D. (1993) "The Conservatives and Training Policy: From a Tripartite to a Neo-Liberal Regime," *Political Studies*, 41: 214–35.

Kingston, P. (2004) "Qualifications Shake Up," *The Guardian*, 13 July.

Koike, K. (1997) *Human Resource Development*, Tokyo: Japan Institute of Labour.

—— (2002) "Intellectual Skills and Competitive Strength: Is a Radical Change Necessary?," *Journal of Education and Work*, 15 (2): 391–408.

Kontiainen, S. (2002) *Dynamic Concept Analysis (DCA): Integrating Information in Conceptual Models*. Helsinki: Helsinki University Press.

Kruse, W. (1986) "On the Necessity of Labour Process Knowledge," in J. Schweitzer (ed.) *Training for a Human Future*, Basle: Weinheim.

Labour Research Department (2003) *Law at Work 2003*, London: Labour Research Department Booklets.

La Valle, I. and Blake, M. (2001) *National Adult Learning Survey (NALS) 2001*, Research Report 321, Nottingham: Department of Education and Skills.

Lave, J. and Wenger, E. (1991) *Situated Learning*, Cambridge: Cambridge University Press.

Learning and Skills Council (2002) *Trust in the Future: The Report of the Bureaucracy Task Force*, Coventry: LSC.

—— (2004) *Extending Trust: The Report of the Bureaucracy Task Force*, Coventry: LSC.

Leont'ev, A. N. (1981) *Problems of the Development of the Mind*, Moscow: Progress Publishers.

Leplat, J. (1990) "Skills and Tacit Skills: A Psychological Perspective," *Applied Psychology: An International Review*, 39 (2): 143–54.

Lewis, P. (2005) "Suppression or Expression: An Exploration of Emotion in a Special Baby Care Unit," *Work, Employment and Society*, 19 (4): 565–82.

Lobato, J. (2003) "How Design Experiments Can Inform a Rethinking of Transfer and Vice Versa," *Educational Researcher*, 32 (1): 21–8.

Mailly, R., Dimmock, S. J., and Sethi, A. S. (1989) *Industrial Relations in the Public Sector*, London: Routledge.

Manpower Services Commission (1981) *The New Training Initiative: An Agenda for Action,* Sheffield: MSC.

Marsick, V. J. and Watkins, K. (1990) *Informal and Incidental Learning in the Workplace*, New York: Routledge.

Matlay, H. (1999) "Employers' Perceptions and Implementation of S/NVQs in Britain: A Critical Overview," *International Journal of Training and Development*, 3 (2): 132–141.

Moustakas, C. (1990) *Heuristic Research: Design, Methodology, and Applications*, London: Sage.

Munro, A. (1999) *Women, Work and Trade Unions*, Mansell: London.

Munro, A. and Rainbird, H. (2000) "The New Unionism and the New Beginning Agenda: UNISON–Employer Partnerships on Workplace Learning in Britain," *British Journal of Industrial Relations*, 38 (2): 223–40.

—— (2002) "Job Change and Workplace Learning in the Public Sector: The Significance of New Technology for Unskilled Work," *New Technology, Work and Employment*, 17 (3): 208–19.

Munro, A., Rainbird, H., and Holly, L. (1997) *Partners in Workplace Learning: A Report on the UNISON–Employer Learning and Development Programme*, London: UNISON.

National Skills Task Force (2000) *Skills for All: Proposals for a National Skills Agenda. Final Report of the National Skills Task Force.* Sudbury: DfEE.

Nonaka, I. and Takeuchi, A. (1995) *The Knowledge Creating Company: How Japanese Companies Create the Dynamics of Innovation*, Oxford: Oxford University Press.

Parker, M. and Slaughter, J. (1988) *Choosing Sides: Unions and the Team Concept*, Detroit, Mich.: Labor Notes.

Peck, J. (1996) *Workplace: The Social Regulation of Labour Markets*, New York: Guildford Press.

Pedlar, M., Burgoyne, J., and Boydell, T. (1991) *The Learning Company*, London: McGraw-Hill.

Performance and Innovation Unit (2001a) *Workforce Development: Analysis*, London: Performance and Innovation Unit.

—— (2001b) *In Demand: Adult Skills in the 21st Century,* London: Performance and Innovation Unit.

Perry, P. J. C. (1976) *The Evolution of British Manpower Policy: From the Statute of Artificers 1593 to the Industrial Training Act 1964*, London: Eyre & Spottiswoode.

Piore, M. and Sabel, C. (1984) *The Second Industrial Divide: Possibilities for Prosperity*, New York: Basic Books.

Power, M. (1997) *The Audit Society: Rituals of Verification*, Oxford: Oxford University Press.

Probert, B. (1999) "Gendered Workers and Gendered Work," in D. Boud and J. Garrick (eds) *Understanding Learning at Work*, London: Routledge.

Pye Tait (2003) *The UK Cleaning Industry 2003 Labour Market Intelligence Update*, Harrogate: Pye Tait.

Raggatt, P. and Williams, S. (1999) *Government, Markets and Vocational Qualifications,* London: London Royal Commission.

Rainbird, H. (1990) *Training Matters: Union Perspectives on Industrial Restructuring and Training*, Oxford: Blackwell.

—— (2005a) "Big on Aspirations, Weak on Delivery," contribution to "Has the Government Got it Right? 21st Century Skills: Realizing Our Potential," *Adults Learning*, 4: 11–12.

—— (2005b) "Workplace Learning in Britain: The Beginning of Institution-alization?," paper prepared for the international seminar "La Formation Professionelle: Systèmes, Innovations et Résultats," Montreal, Canada, June 6–7.

—— (2005c) "A New and Modern Role for Trade Unions? Assessing Partnership Approaches to Lifelong Learning," in M. Martinez Lucio and M. Stuart (eds) *Partnership and Modernization in Employment Relations*, London: Routledge, pp. 46–62.

Rainbird, H., Fuller, A., and Munro, A. (eds) (2004) *Workplace Learning in Context*, London: Routledge.

Rainbird, H., Munro, A., and Senker, P. (2005) "Running Faster to Stay in the Same Place? The Intended and Unintended Consequences of Government Policy for Workplace Learning in the UK," in N. Bascia et al. (eds) *International Handbook of Educational Policy*, 13 (2): 885–901.

Rainbird, H., Munro, A., Holly, L., and Leisten, R. (1999a) "The Future of Work in the Public Sector: Learning and Workplace Inequality," ESRC Future of Work Programme Discussion Paper No. 2, Leeds: University of Leeds.

Rainbird, H., Sutherland, J., Edwards, P. K., Munro, A., and Holly, L. (2003) *Employee Voice and Training at Work: Analysis of Case Studies and WERS 98*. Employment Relations Research Series No. 21, London, Department of Trade and Industry. Online. Available HTTP: <http://www.dti.gov.uk/er/emar>.

Robinson, P. (1996) *Rhetoric and Reality: Britain's New Vocational Qualifications*, London: Centre for Economic Performance, London School of Economics and Political Science.

Royal Commission on Trade Unions and Employers' Associations (1968) *Report of the Royal Commission on Trade Unions and Employers' Associations*, London: HMSO.

Salling Olesen, H. (2001) "Professional Identity as Learning Process Life Histories," in M. C. Broncano et al. (eds) *Adult Education and the Labour Market*, Vol. VI, Xativa: ESREA Adult Education and Labour Market Network.

Scarborough, H., Swan, J., and Preston, J. (1998) *Knowledge Management and the Learning Organization: The IPD Report*, London: Institute of Personnel and Development.

Schmitter, P. and Streeck, W. (eds) (1985) *Private Interest Government: Beyond Market and State*, London: Sage.

Schon, D. (1987) *Educating the Reflective Practitioner*, San Francisco, Calif.: Jossey-Bass.

Scribner, S. and Cole, M. (1973) "Cognitive Consequences of Formal and Informal Education," *Science*, 182: 553–9.

Senge, P. (1990) *The Fifth Discipline: The Art and Practice of the Learning Organization*, New York: Doubleday.

Senker, P. (1992) *Industrial Training in a Cold Climate*, Aldershot: Avebury.

—— (2003) *Research Note for Crossroads*, Northampton: University College Northampton.

—— (2005) "Smothered in Paper: The Fate of Small Voluntary Care Organizations," paper prepared for Conference on Communities and Care: Research, Policy and Practice, Brighton, April 23.

Seymour, D. (2005) "Learning Emotion Rules in Service Organizations: Socialization and Training in the Public House Sector," *Work, Employment and Society* 19 (3): 547–64.

Sfard, A. (1998) "On Two Metaphors for Learning and the Dangers of Choosing Just One," *Educational Researcher*, 27 (2): 4–13.

Solomon, N. (1999) "Culture and Difference in Workplace Learning," in D. Boud and J. Garrick (eds) *Understanding Learning at Work*, London: Routledge.

Storey, J. (ed.) (1989) *New Perspectives on Human Resource Management*, London: Routledge & Kegan Paul.

Strahern, M. (2000) "The Tyranny of Transparency," *British Educational Research Journal*, 26 (3): 309–21.

—— (ed.) (2000) *Audit Cultures: Anthropological Studies in Accountability, Ethics and the Academy*, London: Routledge.

Streeck, W. (1989) "Skills and the Limits to Neo-Liberalism: The Enterprise of the Future as a Place of Learning," *Work, Employment and Society*, 3 (1): 89–104.

Stringer, J. and Richardson, J. (1982) "Policy Stability and Policy Change: Industrial Training 1964–1982," *Public Administration Bulletin*, 39 (1): 22–39.

Sutherland, J. (1998) *Report of the Workplace Learning Task Group: Report to the National Advisory Group on Continuing Education and Lifelong Learning*, London: UNISON.

UNISON (n.d.) *Learning Partnerships in Health and Social Care: An Evaluation of Partnership Initiatives in Health and Social Care*, London: UNISON.

Unwin, L. (1997) "Reforming the Work-Based Route: Problems and Potential for Change," in A. Hodgson and K. Spours (eds) *Dearing and Beyond, 14-19 Qualifications, Frameworks and Systems*, London: Kogan Page.

Unwin, L. and Fuller, A., with Evans, K., Hodkinson, H., Hodkinson, P., Kersh, N., Munro, A., Rainbird, H., and Senker, P. (2003) "Expansive and Restrictive Workplace Learning: Towards an Overarching Conceptual Framework," paper given in SKOPE/Working to Learn Workshop, Warwick, March 14.

Unwin, L., Fuller, A., Turbin, J., and Young, M. (2004) *The Impact of Vocational Qualifications*, Research Report, Nottingham: Department of Education and Skills.

de Ville, O. (1986) *Review of Vocational Qualifications in England and Wales: A Report by the Working Group*, Sheffield and London: Manpower Services Commission/Department of Education and Science.

Vygotsky, L. S. (1978) *Mind in Society*, Cambridge, Mass.: Harvard University Press.

Wenger, E. (1999) *Communities of Practice: Learning, Meaning, and Identity*, Cambridge: Cambridge University Press.

Wertsch, J. V. (1998) *Mind as Action*, Oxford: Oxford University Press.

West, P. and Choueke, R. (2003) "The Alchemy of Action Learning," *Education and Training*, 45 (4): 215–25.

Whitley, R. (2000) *Divergent Capitalisms: The Social Structuring and Change of Business Systems*, Oxford: Oxford University Press.

Winter, R. and Maisch, M. (1996) *Professional Competence and Higher Education: The ASSET Programme*, London: Falmer Press.

Wolcott, H. F. (1994) *Transforming Qualitative Data: Description, Analysis and Interpretation*, London: Sage.

Wolf, A. (1995) *Competence-Based Assessment*, Buckingham: Open University Press.

—— (2002) *Does Education Matter? Myths about Education and Economic Growth*, London: Penguin.

Yoon, J.-H. and Lee, B.-Y. (2005) "Institutional Dynamics of the Vocational Training System in Korea: Systems, Innovations and Results," paper prepared for the international seminar "La Formation Professionelle: Systèmes, Innovations et Résultats," Montreal, Canada, June 6–7.

Young, M. (2004) "Conceptualizing Workplace Knowledge," in H. Rainbird et al. (eds) *Workplace Learning in Context*, London: Routledge.

# Index